To Col. Moynahan's son Beall

"with best wishes
and
warmest of friendship"

"Charlie" Chan

26 Sept 1986

BURMA

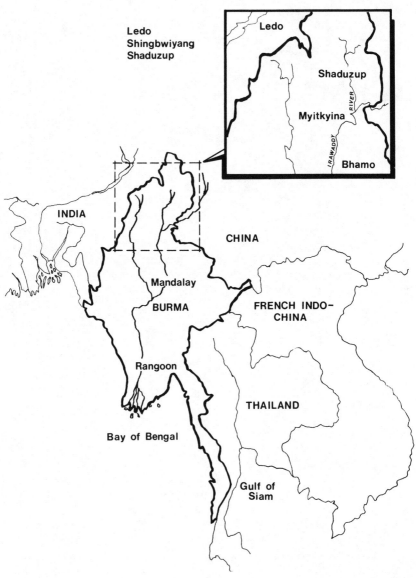

Ledo
Shingbwiyang
Shaduzup

Ledo

Shaduzup

Myitkyina

IRRAWADDY RIVER

Bhamo

INDIA

CHINA

Mandalay

BURMA

FRENCH INDO-
CHINA

Rangoon

THAILAND

Bay of Bengal

Gulf of
Siam

Map by Vic Warren

BURMA
The Untold Story

Won-loy Chan

PRESIDIO

Published by Presidio Press
31 Pamaron Way, Novato CA 94947

Library of Congress Cataloging-in-Publication Data

Chan, Won-loy, 1914–
  Burma, the untold story.

  Includes index.
  1. Chan, Won-loy, 1914– . 2. World War, 1939–1945—Cam-paigns—Burma. 3. World War, 1939–1945—Personal narratives, Amer-ican. 4. Intelligence officers—United States—Biography. 5. United States. Army—Biography. 6. Chinese Americans—Biography. I. Title.
D767.6.c42 1986 940.54′25 86–9504
ISBN 0-89141-266-2

Printed in the United States of America

This book is dedicated to the memory of the late General Joseph W. Stilwell, USA, and to the Asian American officers and men of the Military Intelligence Service who fought in the Asiatic-Pacific campaigns of World War II.

CONTENTS

FOREWORD

A number of books and articles have been published concerning the American participation in the Burma campaigns of World War II. Most focus upon the U.S. commander, General Joseph W. (Vinegar Joe) Stilwell and the strategy and tactics he employed to reoccupy northern Burma. However, there is little that has been written to explain the day-to-day details of the operations, the functioning of the staffs, and the relationships among the diverse commands. This book, by Won-loy Chan, better known as Charlie, is a serious effort to provide insight into the intelligence aspects of some of the more critical operations of the campaign.

I first met Charlie Chan in the fall of 1943 when he joined the intelligence staff of General Stilwell's field-combat headquarters, the Northern Combat Area Command (NCAC). At that time I was in charge of the Office of Strategic Services (OSS) operation in northern Burma, which included espionage, sabotage, guerrilla warfare, and other clandestine activities behind Japanese lines. These operations produced large volumes of information on Japanese locations, operations and activities which were relayed to the intelligence staff at NCAC. To coordinate this intelligence input we established a small group of specialists to work with the NCAC staff. This integrated group worked hand-in-glove under the most adverse conditions presented by the dense jungle and the stifling, humid climate. Nevertheless, they developed a high degree of personal relationships and camaraderie.

Charlie Chan was an important element in all this. Our people soon found that in working with him they were dealing with a true professional. The senior intelligence officer at that time was Col. Joseph W. Stilwell, Jr., but Charlie was the central figure of the intelligence staff. He would accept no piece of information at its face value, it had to be proved. He went to great lengths to assemble all the material and details and then carefully evaluate them in order to convert them into reliable intelligence for use by NCAC as well as by all senior and subordinate commands. This was not an easy task.

Initially, the Chinese divisions which made up the bulk of the Allied combat forces tended to exaggerate the strength of Japanese forces by as much as ten to one; for example an infantry company would be reported as a regiment. As these divisions became experienced in combat the reliability of their intelligence reports greatly improved. Nevertheless, it remained a problem. Aside from the Chinese, numerous reports came in from U.S. forces (principally from Merrill's Marauders), from the British 36th Division, the 3rd Indian Division (Chindits), and from our native Kachin guerrillas.

Added to these was the ever-present problem of working with strange-sounding names: names of towns, mountain ranges, rivers, etc.—names such as Ngumla, Jambu Bum, Koukkwee, to cite but a few. Moreover, northern Burma is predominantly jungle and mountains. There were but few roads or other landmarks to identify a specific location. Under these circumstances, putting all of the bits and pieces of information together was a monumental task. It required a keen mind and a high sense of devotion to duty.

Charlie Chan worked long and hard at his job but he never lost his cheerfulness or his sense of humor. He always had a ready smile and was never too busy to talk with people—an attribute which contributed immeasurably to his success as an intelligence officer.

I feel certain that the readers of this book will note Charlie's fine qualities of friendship and integrity, coupled with his professionalism that is reflected throughout its chapters.

Lt. Gen. W. Ray Peers, USA, Ret.
Kentfield, CA 1 March 1984

Author's Note: General Peers culminated a long and distinguished military career spanning three wars with his investigation of the alleged My Lai massacre in Vietnam. He was the author of the *My Lai Inquiry,* based on that investigation. He was also the author of *Behind Burma Lines,* as well as numerous professional articles.

General Peers died on 6 April 1984 at Letterman Army Medical Center, Presidio of San Francisco, California.

ACKNOWLEDGEMENTS

I wish to acknowledge the contributions made by Grant Hirabayashi, Toichi "Tom" Ichimura, and Yasuharu "Yas" Koike in providing anecdotal material; to retired Colonels Stuart Crossman and George Moynahan, Jr., and to former army nurses Lorraine Craig Dowling and Grace Kindig Coulson for supplying long forgotten details; to the National Archives for maps; to the U.S. Army Photo Service for selected photos; and to the National Records Center for the use of their official files of the Hukawng Valley and Myitkyina campaigns.

A very special acknowledgement to my wartime comrade, my good friend, retired Army Colonel James D. Holland.

PART I
HOW IT ALL BEGAN

An autographed photograph of the late General Joseph W. Stilwell, presented to the Chan family in 1945. Photo was taken in 1944.

Capt. Won-loy Chan greets Gen. Joseph Stilwell at the Artillery School, Fort Sill, Oklahoma, March 1945.

General Stilwell greets Capt. "Charlie" Chan at Fort Sill, Oklahoma, March 1945.

Col. Won-loy Chan retires from the Army of the United States at Fort Myer, Virginia, 26 April 1968

California to India

December 7, 1941, "a day that shall live in infamy." I was in Tulare, California. A twenty-seven year old Chinese American, holding a second lieutenant's commission in the United States Army Reserve. A year later I would be on active duty with the Army of the United States in far off India and Burma, serving as a combat intelligence officer on the staff of Gen. Joseph W. (Vinegar Joe) Stilwell and concurrently as a Japanese language officer with Chinese, American, British, and Indian troops in that all but forgotten World War II theater of operations known as the CBI (China-Burma-India).

My father, Chan Jing-hing, came to the United States from the little village of Sam Shui near Canton in southeast China. He and his brother entered San Francisco as merchants through the old immigration station at the Pacific Mail Steamship Dock on the Embarcadero around the turn of the century. He settled in San Francisco and remained there until the earthquake and fire of 1906. Then after a few years in Watsonville, he married my mother and they moved to Marshfield and then to North Bend, Oregon where Dad opened a general store. I was born in North Bend in 1914.

I was one of four boys and two girls born to Jing-hing and Mae Lee Chan. We grew up in the Scandinavian American community of North Bend, attending American schools. But my father insisted that we not forget our Chinese heritage, language, and culture. He required that we speak Cantonese at home and that we memorize the "Trimetrical Classic" and the "1,000 Word Classic," which we did while stocking the shelves and sorting the vegetables in his store! I can still recite most of them today.

After I completed grammar school in North Bend, my father sent me to San Francisco where I attended Francisco Junior High School in the daytime while continuing my Chinese education at the Nam Kue Chinese School at night. I later returned to North Bend where I graduated from high school in 1931. After working in Dad's store for another year to acquire a stake, I applied for and was accepted by Stanford University in the class of 1936, the only Chinese American in that class. Along with my degree in economics I took ROTC and received a commission in the U.S. Army Field Artillery Reserve in June 1936. I entered law school at Stanford in the fall of 1937 but the death of my elder brother caused me to take a leave of absence to assist my parents with the family business. Since the Sino-Japanese War was in full swing, I also wanted to play an active roll in helping the Chinese, which I did as a volunteer worker with the American Bureau for Medical Aid to China.

Immediately following Pearl Harbor, I received orders calling me to active duty and directing me to report to Camp Roberts, California, a replacement training center, not later than 15 January 1942. However, on 13 January these orders were amended and I went instead to the Presidio of San Francisco and the Office of the Assistant Chief of Staff for Intelligence (G-2), Fourth U.S. Army, from which I was further assigned to the newly organized Fourth Army Intelligence School to become a Japanese intelligence specialist. Because I was concurrently working for the G-2, my co-workers, instructors, and fellow students dubbed me "Charlie" Chan and that name has stuck with me ever since. I accepted it then and continue to wear it now with pride because I know of the affection and respect with which it was bestowed.

For the first five months of 1942, we studied hard at Crissy Field but in May 1942, following President Roosevelt's Executive Order #9066, the remnants of our first class were relocated to Camp Savage, Minnesota and renamed the Military Intelligence Service Language School (MISLS). At the same time, the course was expanded so that in addition to spoken and written Japanese, we also studied general intelligence subjects.

For reasons still unknown to me, I graduated from MISLS on 10 November 1942—one month ahead of my class—and concurrently received orders to report to the Port of Embarcation at Fort Mason, California for further travel to an undisclosed destination.

I spent six days of leave with my family, which passed all too quickly, then reported to Fort Mason where, along with 223 others ranging in rank from second lieutenant to colonel, I found myself being processed for immediate shipment overseas. I was the only one from MISLS and the only Japanese intelligence specialist.

We sailed at dawn on 8 December 1942. Our ship was a former luxury liner, the SS *Île de France,* that had been interned in New York Harbor, stripped of its opulent fittings, and converted to a troop carrier. That night at dinner I met the other Chinese American officers aboard. Some I knew from San Francisco; Lieutenants John Chew Young and Will Win Lee were also former residents of Chinatown and graduates of Stanford and ROTC. (Two doctors, Captain Edwin Owyang and Lieutenant Albert Young, also from Chinatown, returned from the Pacific War and today practice medicine in San Francisco.)

The first day out of San Francisco we all received orders to learn Mandarin Chinese. Our destination had to be China! U.S. Army Cpl. Charles F. Hockett, who held a Ph.D. in Oriental languages from Yale, instructed us along with two civilian employees from the War Department. We studied Mandarin for three hours a day, six days a week as we steamed across the Pacific. On 13 December 1942, six days out of San Francisco, we raised Diamond Head and sailed into Pearl Harbor, Hawaii, scene of America's worst naval disaster. It was a sight I'll never forget. We stayed at Pearl less than twenty-four hours, taking on fuel and supplies. No one got to go ashore except a few members of the crew and the official couriers. We visited America's island paradise from the boat deck!

On 14 December we steamed out of Pearl Harbor on a southwest course for Australia and New Zealand. We sailed into Wellington, New Zealand on Christmas Eve, seventeen days out of San Francisco.

In Wellington we were granted shore leave, our first chance to get our feet on terra firma after almost three weeks at sea. The people of Wellington, whose sons, brothers, husbands and fathers were fighting in North Africa, welcomed us with open arms. Many families invited us into their homes for Christmas dinners. Wellington's Chinatown—when it was known that there were Chinese American officers aboard on their way to chase the Japanese out of China—really went all out for us. We spent Christmas Eve at a Chinese banquet complete with flowery speeches to which we responded in kind while Coca-Cola (and stronger spirits) flowed.

Shore leave passed all too quickly and on 27 December we sailed out of Wellington Harbor. On 14 January 1943, thirty-eight days out of San Francisco, we tied up at a dock in Bombay, India. After one day of orientation we got our assignments. I drew a place called Ramgarh in eastern India where General Stilwell was training Chinese troops. We left the SS *Île de France* and boarded a funny looking little narrow-gauge Indian train. It took us more than three days and nights to cross the central plains of India until on 20 January 1943 our little train rolled into the station at Ramgarh.

Ramgarh and the Chih Hui Pu

In a spirit of allied cooperation, the British in India had offered Ramgarh to General Stilwell for the rehabilitation and retraining of the Chinese divisions—or rather the remnants of them—that he had led out of Burma at the end of the disastrous First Burma campaign. At one time a British-Indian army post, Ramgarh had been converted to a prisoner-of-war facility for Italians that the British had picked up in North Africa. Located in Bihar Province about two hundred miles northwest of Calcutta, it wasn't too bad a camp, as camps go. The mosquitos weren't as numerous or vicious as they were in other parts of India or in Burma. The malaria rate was low. There were railhead facilities, woefully inadequate by American standards but better than average for India. The campsite boasted varied terrain and did have firing ranges for small arms, mortars, automatic weapons, and light artillery. The permanent buildings were one-story whitewashed structures made of an adobelike mud with either rough tile or thatched roofs. The thatch played host to a myriad of insects, small rodents, and an occasional cobra. There weren't nearly enough of these structures to house all the Chinese troops, so a number of British double-walled tents dotted the landscape.

On 29 June 1942, Chiang Kai-shek gave his approval to Ramgarh and it became officially known as the Ramgarh Training Center as well as the headquarters for the *Chih Hui Pu* (Chinese Army in India).

General Stilwell, who started out as Chiang's chief of staff, wound up with more hats than Hedda Hopper. As deputy commander of the Southeast Asia Command (SEAC), he reported to Admiral Lord Louis Mountbatten in Kandy, Ceylon; as commander of the China-Burma-India (CBI) theater of operations, he reported to President Roosevelt through General Marshall in Washington; as chief of staff and later as commander of all Chinese forces in India-Burma, he reported to Generalissimo Chiang Kai-shek in Chungking, China. His Chih Hui Pu staff was headed by U.S. Brig. Gen. Haydon L. Boatner and consisted of Chinese officers and enlisted men and their American counterparts. Boatner and his principal staff officers were American but the headquarters, the Chih Hui Pu, was legally constituted and diplomatically recognized as Chinese.

The Chinese Army structure allowed for little in the way of logistical support or medical units. At Ramgarh this support was mostly supplied by the British through their Indian Army and by some American medical and signal units. Unit administration, discipline, provision of replacements and fillers were all Chinese responsibilities. Although training was theoretically carried out by Chinese officers, each unit from separate company size on up had an American advisor or liaison officer. Needless to say this polyglot mishmash created many problems. Initially, at least, solutions were few.

Except for a few regular army officers such as the Stilwells and Boatner, Chinese was not a popular language among our professional military men. The call up of vast numbers of reservists in 1941 and 1942 didn't do much to alleviate this communications problem. The universities and colleges from whence most reserve officers came, with very few exceptions, did not offer courses in Oriental languages. There weren't many Chinese or Asian American reserve officers, and what few there were usually held commissions in the technical services. Assignments for liaison (advisory) duty with our Chinese allies were based on military training, experience, and education; there was no time to send officers to a language school. What to do? Enter the Fan I Kuan—the Chinese interpreter. Young Chinese, usually without military background or training, they were either volunteers or drafted into the Chinese Army as officers for the sole purpose of bridging the language gap. The contribution to training, camaraderie, and Chinese American understanding made by the Fan I Kuan was immeasurable. Many a friendship begun in India between a Chinese and an American continues to flourish today.

General Stilwell had led the remnants of the Chinese 22nd and 38th divisions out of Burma in May 1942. By the time I arrived at Ramgarh some seven months later, the Ramgarh Training Center and the Chih Hui Pu were in full operation. A number of basic problems had been solved and the Chinese American staff of the Chih Hui Pu was functioning. The retraining of what was left of the 22nd and 38th divisions and the training of replacements and fillers as well as newly organized support units was well underway as was planning for the Second Burma campaign. In preparing the plan, it had been decided to adopt Chinese Army staff organization and procedures. While this was tough on our Americans, who had been schooled in U.S. Army procedures, it was more readily understood by the Chinese who made up the bulk of the staff and by the Chinese unit commanders who would have to implement the plan.

All orders, memos, plans, and other documents were written in English and then translated into Chinese for dissemination. Conversely, Chinese unit reports to the Chih Hui Pu were written in Chinese and then translated into English for the benefit of the American staff and for the record. Everything was done on Chih Hui Pu letterheads and with General Stilwell's Chinese chop at the bottom to make it official. Paperwork in any army is voluminous. In General Stilwell's Chinese Army in India it was doubly so.

I had learned both written and spoken Japanese and was considered a Japanese intelligence specialist. Nevertheless, I found myself initially assigned to the Chih Hui Pu G-4 (logistics) section. On 21 January 1943, the day after my arrival at Ramgarh, I reported to General Boatner for a personal interview. He told me that he'd have to consult with the CBI theater G-2 concerning my permanent assignment but that in the meantime, I'd be placed with the G-4. Later I was informed that I would eventually be assigned to the G-2 section at General Stilwell's combat (Forward) headquarters somewhere near the India-Burma border.

I had had no logistics experience but after two months on the job at Ramgarh, I found that I had not only learned the nomenclature of military items used by the Chinese, I had become familiar with the Chinese Tables of Organization and Equipment (TO&Es). Even more important, I had met and worked with many Chinese officers and enlisted men from the Chinese 22nd and 38th divisions with whom I would later fight side by side.

I quickly settled into a routine. My quarters weren't bad, and in the British manner an Indian bearer brought me tea in the morning, took care of my laundry, and kept the room reasonably clean. The G-4 office was in a long, low building with large open windows. No glass. You just put up the shutters when it rained, which it did frequently. Overhead fans stirred the stale hot air but also made it difficult to keep papers on the desks. After an American breakfast at 0700, I was at my desk at 0730 and except for a lunch break, worked steadily until 1700, usually going back for a few more hours after the evening meal. The real war seemed a long way off until one afternoon about 1430 hours the air-raid siren shrieked and somebody yelled, "This ain't no drill." Americans and Chinese alike exited the building in a hurry, jumping down into slit trenches that had been dug as make-shift air-raid shelters throughout the center. We stayed in the trenches about half an hour until the all clear sounded. I didn't see any planes or hear any for that matter, but I guess they were up there somewhere. After my twelve to fourteen hour days poring over the Chinese Tables of Organization and Equipment, even an air raid was welcome, es-pecially when it turned out to be all air and no raid.

Early in 1943 we began to get the Chinese corps and divisional support units ready to move to the forward areas, along with some units of the 38th Division. Some of the officers from GA-214 would go with them as advisors.

Being a Chinese American officer at the Chih Hui Pu did have some advantages. I was more readily accepted by the Chinese and I could converse with them—to a degree that is, since my Chinese was in the Cantonese dialect while most of them spoke Mandarin. All of them, however, wanted to learn English, while I was anxious to im-prove my knowledge of Mandarin, begun in those classes aboard the *Île de France*. To this end I started a class among the Chinese officers of the Chih Hui Pu where I taught them American English and they taught me Mandarin Chinese!

One of the Chinese enlisted men, a Sergeant Ho from the G-4, invited me to play badminton. The Chinese excel at this game and I think he wanted to test me. We played for about an hour and my badminton training from San Francisco's Chinatown paid off. I beat him. He was a good loser and invited me to dinner at a Chinese res-taurant. It was great to enjoy a Chinese meal again and the food was so excellent it made me homesick for San Francisco.

The G-3 of the Chih Hui Pu had the task in January and February 1943 of developing new Tables of Organization and Equipment (TO&Es) for the reconstituted Chinese divisions plus the support units they would need. These TO&Es would also be used for the additional twenty-eight divisions General Stilwell hoped to get from the gener-alissimo at some later date. The 22nd and 38th Divisions, when they were in Burma in early 1942, were organized entirely along Chinese lines. The first Ramgarh reorganization plan converted the divisions into six artillery and three infantry (heavy weapons) battalions. After retraining they were to have been flown over the Hump to become part of the thirty-division Y Force in China. However, because Chiang Kai-shek was unable to provide sufficient manpower for the thirty-division force that the United States had agreed to equip and train in China, the first Ramgarh plan changed shortly before I arrived there. General Stilwell decided to develop the 22nd and 38th divisions into strong strike forces with the mission of retaking north Burma and spearheading the opening of the Ledo (later the Stilwell) Road. It took all his persuasive powers to get Chiang's acceptance of this plan, but Stilwell succeeded.

Support units such as medics, communications troops, and the like had to be supplied from Stilwell's meager resources in the CBI or organized and trained from scratch using Chinese fillers. Stilwell supplied all the medics and most of the communications troops, since there wasn't time for training.

Equipment was a different story. When the 22nd and 38th divisions retreated out of Burma in early 1942, they, like most retreating armies throughout history, left behind much of their equipment, weapons, and ammunition. The United States had been pouring supplies, arms, and ammunition into China to equip Chiang's forces. Most of this had gone by way of the Burma Road from the railhead at Lashio to Kunming, Yunnan Province, in southwest China. When the Japanese took Rangoon this supply line shut down leaving only the airlift over the Hump, which in the beginning could only handle about 5,000 tons a month—hardly enough to take care of the needs of General Chennault's Flying Tiger air force. General Stilwell's logistical problems were almost insurmountable. The C-46 and C-47 aircraft that flew over the Hump couldn't take heavy artillery, so these items, almost thirty-divisions worth, had to be diverted to depots in India. To reequip the approximately 9,000 Chinese that wound up in Ramgarh in May 1942, in addition to the roughly 10,000 replacements and fillers flown in from China, Stilwell had a surplus of artillery and heavy weapons but a shortage of small arms. With a full-scale war going on in the Pacific and in north Africa, with training for invasion going on in the United States and in England, the CBI was not only a low logistical priority (it was #9 of 9), it was also at the end of the war's longest supply line. Our job was to tailor the Chinese units at Ramgarh to the equipment and weapons available.

To understand the importance of north Burma, you have to take a look at the big picture. The President was committed to keeping

China in the war. To accomplish this, Roosevelt had to accept Chiang Kai-shek as an equal, as he had accepted Churchill and Stalin. Chiang insisted on receiving his share of the Allied arsenal, which was supplied almost solely by the United States. The problem was to get his share to him with the entire east coast of China and most of Southeast Asia in the hands of the Japanese, and now the Burma Road closed. The Ledo, later to become Stilwell, Road through north Burma by way of Myitkyina to link up with the northern end of the Burma Road was the answer.

The British wanted Burma back as part of the Empire. General Stilwell wanted it back because "we got the hell beat out of us." The real reason for retaking Burma was to open the Stilwell Road.

By mid-February 1943 we were getting ready to begin the Second Burma campaign. The new TO&Es were complete and had been implemented. We had issued new equipment to the 22nd and 38th divisions, the motorized artillery, 10th and 12th Engineer regiments, and other support troops. General Stilwell, accompanied by Gen. Ho Ying-chin, Minister of War, and T. V. Soong, Financial Advisor to the Generalissimo, were here to review the troops. Colonel Eckert (my boss) had just returned from CBI headquarters in New Delhi to announce that he was leaving us to assume command of the Ledo Sector Forces.

It was a Red Letter Day for me. Or so I thought. A Japanese spy was captured on the train that came into Ramgarh from the west. He was turned over to the Chinese Military Police (CMP), who didn't have any Japanese linguists, so this Chinese American graduate of MISLS was called to interrogate the prisoner. I caught a jeep ride to the CMP headquarters, all set to put my knowledge of Japanese and interrogation procedures to work. "What prisoner?" asked the Chinese MP lieutenant. "We don't have any Japanese here." I never did find out who had called me, and I never did locate a prisoner to interrogate. Knowing the Chinese, if they did have one, they probably took him out and shot him.

The pace continued to accelerate in March. Some of the Chinese troops had already gone forward into Assam near the Burma border. More VIPs kept coming to Ramgarh to review the troops. My work was purely routine. My days were spent at G-4 of the Chih Hui Pu while my nights found me looking for new Chinese restaurants in the area. I also played Ma-jong, Ping-Pong, and poker with my Chinese and American friends and became an expert at all three. Mail from home, the great morale builder, was sparse and slow in arriving. The spring monsoons began and it was hot, hot, hot.

Margherita and Mile Mark 5 1/2

On 2 April 1943 General Stilwell issued orders establishing his Forward or Combat Headquarters. Known as Headquarters, Combat Troops, Ledo Sector, it was initially located at Margherita in Assam, India. On 23 May 1943 headquarters was moved to its permanent location at the 5 1/2 Mile Mark on Tokyo Road in northern Assam near the Burma border, where it stayed until moved to Myitkyina on 18 August 1944. General Stilwell's promised "return to Burma" was about to begin.

By this time, parts of the Chinese 38th Division were already in the Assam area. Japanese forces had been sighted north of Shingbwi-yang towards Tagap where their presence posed a threat to American support forces and facilities in Assam. Chinese troops were needed to protect them. Also, the terrain in Assam was well suited for advanced jungle-combat training.

On 2 April 1943 by verbal order of Gen. Stilwell, I accompanied General Boatner and Col. Robert M. Cannon on detached service to Ledo, India. Pretty fast company for me, but apparently I was going to be part of the intelligence staff at General Stilwell's combat headquarters. We flew out of Ramgarh (Ranchi) at 0900 hours in General Stilwell's personal plane. The weather was miserable. Rain, fog, low clouds, and *cold*. The monsoons had begun. It was a bumpy flight that took about six-and-a-half hours to reach Chabua in Assam, where we ate dinner at the Army Air Corps mess and were given makeshift beds for the night.

On 3 April we rose at dawn and after a hurried breakfast I joined General Boatner and Colonel Cannon for a spine-jarring ride to Ledo and then on to Margherita in jeeps with Chinese drivers. It was jungle country with lush vegetation. We drove through a number of tea plantations where Indian women, bare to the waist in the hot, humid air, were picking tea leaves. After five to six hours of being bounced over a dirt road that more nearly resembled a hacked-out jungle trail, we finally got to Margherita. We were met there by Lt. Col. Edward J. McNally, Ledo Sector G-2, and soon to be my boss. Colonel McNally briefed us on the current situation. Chinese troops had clashed with the Japanese just a few miles away at Nathkaw. Two weeks ago Japanese planes had bombed Margherita but inflicted only minor damage. Our Chinese ack-ack gunners shot down two confirmed and one possible. Listening to Colonel McNally's report, I got the feeling that I was really at the front, six months after graduating from MISLS. Now I could put that Camp Savage training to good use.

Margherita was a desolate spot in the jungle northwest of Ledo in Assam. Nothing but tall trees that blocked out the sun, rotting vegetation, mud, leeches, rain, and snakes. We were temporarily set up in a Dak bungalow located on a small rise that provided some drainage. Chinese and Americans worked side by side. We slept in tents nearby and took our meals in a larger tent where Indian cooks sweated over charcoal fires. We were a small staff: only five Americans and five Chinese. Colonel McNally acted as both G-1 and G-2, with myself as Assistant G-2. Two ex-officio members of our staff are worthy of mention. "Major" John Day, an overseas Chinese (I never did learn his Chinese name) who had been in northeast India and Burma for many (he wouldn't say how many) years, was hired by Colonel McNally as an interpreter-translator. He wore U.S. Army khakis and referred to himself as Major. Somewhere between forty and fifty years of age, short and stocky, his face burned dark by the tropical sun, Day was reticent about his background and personal life. He spoke both Mandarin and Cantonese Chinese plus Urdu, Burmese, English, and a number of the Hill Tribe dialects. The Major was a mystery man and an indispensable adjunct to our staff. Want to know where to find various types of food for our polyglot collection of troops and native workers? Ask John Day. Want to buy jade or rubies? Ask John Day. Want that "Burma Girl a sittin'?" Ask John Day.

The British had governed Burma from the midnineteenth century, first as a colonial possession and later (since 1937) as a sort of dominion, though Burma never did attain full dominion status. The country was divided into a number of districts, with a district commissioner in charge of each; and depending on the district's size, population and economic importance, there would also be a staff of sorts to assist the commissioner. The Englishmen who held the position of commissioners in the British Colonial Service were indeed a breed apart. Usually they entered the colonial service directly out of college and then spent the rest of their adult lives in the far-flung, remote outposts of the British Empire.

Capt. C. Evans Darlington had been the district commissioner for the Hukawng Valley of Burma for a number of years before the conquest of Burma by the Japanese between 1941 and 1942. He knew the valley as no other man did. He spoke the languages of the tribes that inhabited north Burma and through years of diligent effort had gained the tribes' respect and loyalty, particularly the Kachins, the area's dominant tribe. By British custom all colonial-service officers held reserve army commissions and when Darlington was forced to flee Burma for India in early 1942, he was ordered to active duty as a captain in the British-Indian Army and assigned as the British liaison officer to the Chih Hui Pu and later to the U.S. Northern Combat Area Command (NCAC). In his late thirties, Darlington was of medium height and build. His dark brown hair was curly and he sported a thin, well-trimmed mustache. His British accent was most pronounced, which didn't seem to affect his ability to converse with the Kachins in their own dialect. His knowledge of the Hukawng Valley and its inhabitants was invaluable to the Chih Hui Pu and later the NCAC staff, both of whom consulted him frequently. I spent many hours with Darlington in the Fall of 1943, during which time he taught me a great deal about the Hukawng Valley that I couldn't have learned any other way. When weather permitted we drove by jeep as far as we could down the Stilwell Road, stopping at the villages along the way. At each one Darlington would introduce me to the village headman. We would take tea or some other liquid refreshment and Darlington would explain who and what I was. This was necessary if I was to ever get any cooperation later, since the experiences the natives had had both with the Japanese and later some of the Chinese troops were not conducive to making friends. These trips also gave me the opportunity to observe the living habits and customs of the Kachins. For his help, counsel, advice, and all-around value to the U.S. forces, Darlington was later awarded the Legion of Merit by our government.

No matter where I've been in this world, I've always managed to find Chinese food. To paraphrase Kipling, the sun never sets on a Chinese restaurant. Of course the restaurants of my youth in San Francisco's Chinatown—the Far East, Hang Far Low, and Sam Wo among others—were truly outstanding. Nevertheless, I was pleased to find that an enterprising overseas Chinese had opened a Cantonese style restaurant in Ledo, where I enjoyed some excellent meals. It wasn't a very impressive establishment: a rundown bungalow which doubled as living quarters for the owner and his large family. The largest room had been converted to the restaurant dining room. It had several long tables like those you'd find at outdoor picnic sites in the United States with long benches on both sides. The floor was dirt, pounded hard. Two bare, unshaded forty-watt bulbs hung from the ceiling. The only decoration was a small, silk-embroidered Chinese tiger on one wall. Near the door that led to the lean-to kitchen was another wooden table holding cracked and chipped teapots and cups, chopsticks, and bottles of soy sauce. The kitchen had been built against the outside wall of the bungalow. Two cement stoves held large woks in which most of the cooking was done over wood fires. There was an assortment of Chinese utensils—some old, some obviously handmade and primitive, some classics—hanging on the walls. The heavy chopping block held knives and the ever present *choy doh* (the Chinese big knife) without which a Chinese cook could not prepare a meal. From the corrugated roof of the lean-to hung dried herbs and vegetables, barbecued strips of meat, and of course, garlic. The hygiene and surroundings weren't up to San Francisco standards but the meals were excellent.

Another Chinese restaurant I enjoyed was in the "sin city" of Dibrugarh, a few hours north of Margherita by jeep. Since the town was near our air bases and support facilities and frequented by our GIs, trips there were necessary! John Day introduced me to the Chinese restaurant owner on our first trip. The owner spoke Cantonese so we got along very well and a rapport was quickly established. The food was excellent and I got the feeling that I had an additional safe haven if I needed it. Both restaurants were excellent intelligence sources and their Chinese owners provided more information about that part of India than all the combined military systems of the American, Chinese, and British intelligence services put together!

On 4 April 1943 Colonel McNally assigned me to mind the store, so to speak, while he spent most of his time up front. I was to keep up with the intelligence situation using maps, charts, captured documents, prisoner interrogations, and personal visits to frontline units when time permitted and also to write the situation reports (SITREPS) for combat headquarters. Being bilingual was probably my most valuable asset in this assignment. The small Chinese G-2 staff of the Chih Hui Pu worked in the same small bungalow, and we quickly established an informal rapport. Information flowed freely between us, and as a result I was better able to keep our headquarters advised. My first act was to post on our map the arrival of the 112th Regiment of the Chinese 38th Division which had pulled in from Ramgarh.

In preparation for the coming offensive, General Boatner got me working closely with Capt. John Wilson, a British officer who was with the Kachin Levies. Captain Wilson, like Captain Darlington, had a vast knowledge of the area.

On 4 April I also received my baptism as a G-2. I learned that Indian units—two companies—stationed at Shamdak-ku and Hkalak Ga had withdrawn to the north when attacked by a Japanese force estimated at about 500 strong. (I learned later that the Japanese only stayed a couple of days and then the Indians reoccupied their positions.) At the same time a force of about 150 Japanese engaged Chinese troops from the 114th Regiment at Nathkaw and Nathkaw Sakan. The Chinese threw back the attack. This was the first taste of combat for the 1st Battalion of the 114th and, according to reports, they acquitted themselves well against the Japanese, who were part of the battle-tested and blooded 56th Regiment now part of the Japanese 18th Division based at Myitkyina. The Chinese lost six men killed in a skirmish about twenty-five miles from headquarters. They allowed themselves to be overrun by a Japanese raiding party while guarding a support radio station.

In a valley east of Hukawng near Sumprabum, Japanese forces attacked Kachin Levies guarding the approach to the Fort Hertz (Putao) Air Station, a small detachment of the U.S. Army Air Corps that provided navigational aid and maintained an emergency landing field for the C-46s and C-47s that flew the Hump. The Kachins beat off the attackers and the station was safe for the moment.

Being the only Japanese intelligence specialist around, I got a call on the morning of 9 April to come to the airfield at Kanjikoa, about sixty rugged miles from headquarters. At Kanjikoa I was shown papers and maps from the wreckage of a Japanese reconnaissance plane shot down as it flew over the airfield. The pilot was killed, but the plane did not burn. The maps and charts recovered not only gave the pilot's flight plan, they pinpointed the location of every Japanese airfield and emergency landing strip in Burma! I stayed overnight at Kanjikoa, returning to Margherita on 10 April. In my report I strongly recommended that at least one and preferably two Japanese American linguists from MISLS be assigned to our headquarters as soon as possible. I could, as I did this time, pinch-hit in an emergency, but I knew that we were going to need Japanese linguists full time as the campaign progressed. Eight months passed before our priority got us a language team. In the interim, this Chinese American provided the Combat Forward Headquarters with its only Japanese language capability. The first two-man Japanese American MISLS team arrived in December 1943.

The CBI theater should be called the international theater, with its American GIs, Chinese Pings, British Tommies, Indian troops (both Hindu and Muslim), Gurkhas from Nepal, New Zealanders, Burmese nurses of Dr. (Lt. Col.) Gordon Seagraves' hospital unit, and Kachin Levies, mountain tribesmen from the Kachin Hills commanded by British officers. The logistics were formidable: the Muslim Indians wouldn't eat pork; the Hindu Indians wouldn't eat beef; the British and Chinese wanted their tea; we Americans wanted our coffee; the Gurkhas and the Kachin Levies had their special diets; and so it went. Our weapons, especially small arms, were of different calibers, making ammunition resupply a problem. At least the units all used the ubiquitous jeep!

The Albacore Plan

In May 1943 the spring monsoons arrived. It rained. Every day it rained. Nothing ever got fully dry and mildew was the name of the game. Leather rots; your skin softens then splits and bleeds; you get jock itch from the wetness and sweat and Dhobi itch from whatever the Indian Dhobi Wallahs use to get clothes clean—clean but never dry.

By mid-May planning for the Second Burma campaign was well

underway at Mile Mark 5 1/2. On 26 May 1943 General Boatner issued a memorandum: "Based on available information and with as much detail as conditions will permit, draw up tactical plans for operations in this Sector."

Boatner went on to outline the two missions that became the Albacore Plan: first, to protect the Ledo base and the road construction it supported; and second, to recapture Myitkyina and reestablish land communications with China.

"Based on available information," General Boatner had said. We didn't have a whole helluva lot and our G-2 section consisted of Colonel McNally and me. Since McNally was also the G-1, it fell to me to do most of the G-2 work.

Collecting enemy intelligence—how to do it, collate it, pass it on, and effectively use it in preparing tactical plans—is taught in all U.S. Army schools. The problem was that the textbooks and teachers at MISLS didn't, perhaps couldn't, take into account the myriad nationalities we'd be working with in the CBI: the diversity of systems; the languages spoken and written—English, Chinese, Tamil, Hindi, Burmese, and various tribal dialects that had no written form; and the multiplicity of command channels. We had ours, the Chinese had theirs, and the Chih Hui Pu was supposed to meld these two. The British also had their own system and except at the lower levels of command weren't too anxious to share their intelligence with us. Nevertheless, we tried. While the Chinese troops fighting Japanese forces did not filter back good intelligence when left to their own devices, these units were accompanied by some American liaison personnel and so I was able to develop a pretty good order of battle for the Japanese units that confronted us—an essential to tactical planning. Indoctrinating newly assigned American personnel was also essential and we did this for all newcomers at our headquarters before they joined their Chinese units.

Coordination with higher and other headquarters was also necessary, so on 4 June I was ordered to TDY in New Delhi with Stilwell's rear echelon headquarters. Maj. Joseph Boyes, although a medical officer, was temporarily attached to our G-2 section and he accompanied me. Boyes and I drove by jeep to Chabua where we stayed overnight. On the way we stopped at the Kanjikoa Airfield where I delivered orders to the commander of the 51st Fighter Group to bomb everything south of Shingbwiyang.

We took off from Chabua at 0830 hours on 6 June and landed at Dum Dum Airfield near Calcutta three-and-one-half hours later. From there we flew to Ranchi near Ramgarh and at 1930 hours, 11 hours out of Chabua, we finally touched down at the Agra Airfield close by the Taj Mahal.

We rose early on 7 June and made the short flight to New Delhi. What a contrast to Margherita and Mile Mark 5 1/2 deep in the jungles of Assam: wide, tree-lined boulevards; hundreds of motor vehicles of all shapes and sizes—British lorries, American two-and-one-half ton trucks, jeeps, and taxis by the dozens. The taxis seemed to be mostly American made Buick touring cars from the 1920s. All were driven by fierce looking bearded and turbaned Sikhs who apparently thought a motor car had only two accessories: the gas pedal and an old-fashioned Klaxon horn. With their foot on the former and their right hand squeezing the bulb of the latter, they careened through the streets with reckless abandon. The literally thousands of *gharries* (horse-drawn open carriages), donkey carts, bullock carts, and man-powered rickshaws added to the confusion. As if all this weren't enough, Indian cattle, sacred to the Hindus, roamed the streets at will. So did thousands of pedestrians who paid little or no attention to the brilliantly uniformed and dignified Sikh policemen who professed to direct and control traffic with stately waves of their hands.

Major Boyes and I were given quarters at the beautiful old Imperial Hotel where I luxuriated in a long shower before changing into fresh khakis and reporting to General Stilwell's principal headquarters in India. It was strange after months in the jungles of Assam to see hundreds of American officers and non-coms bustling about in starched, pressed khakis, clean-shaven, with shined shoes, and polished brass. Boyes and I presented our orders to the headquarters adjutant, who sent us directly to the offices of the G-2. We got a good initial briefing and in turn gave a first-hand account of how things were at the Burma front. We also got the VIP treatment: full-scale briefing in the supersecret War Room by General Stilwell's briefing officer. It was interesting to see the big picture and to realize what a small cog we were in General Stilwell's big wheel. The public relations officer briefed us on the complex relationships in Stilwell's many-faceted command, and we had the opportunity to talk with Toby Wiant of the Associated Press. In true war correspondent fashion, he asked us a lot of questions we could not answer.

We spent ten busy, interesting, and profitable days at Stilwell's New Delhi headquarters. I saw Vinegar Joe once or twice in the hallways, but didn't get to speak with him. He looked preoccupied and just a bit tired. I could understand why after being in New Delhi just a few hours especially when realizing he must go through the same thing both at SEAC in Ceylon with Mountbatten and with the Generalissimo in Chungking. Col. Frank Merrill, one of a handful of American officers who had studied in Japan before the war, dropped into the G-2 office. A quiet, soft-spoken, pipe-smoking man, Colonel Merrill had walked out of Burma with General Stilwell at the end of the disastrous First Burma campaign and it was easy to tell from his conversation that, like General Stilwell, he was anxious to get back.

Ten days and 2,000 flying miles later we got back to Mile Mark 5 1/2 on 15 June. It had been a worthwhile trip; we had shared a lot of good intelligence. I had also developed a better understanding of the problems facing higher headquarters and could only hope that they now had some appreciation of our problems. One thing was certain, they didn't have the Japanese Army, mosquitos, leeches, cobras, and mud!

July and August of 1943 were busy months for our combat headquarters and for me. We stuck with our present mission, protecting the Ledo Base and the road construction, while continuing to plan for our future mission, recapturing Myitkyina and opening the road to China. By September General Boatner's staff had grown from the original five to twenty-four. In our G-2 section Lt. Harvey Patton replaced Major Boyes, who went back to his medical duties. Lieutenant Patton was a Coast Artillery officer and like Boyes was with us on a temporary basis. He stayed for about two months. It seemed as though I was to provide the continuity in the G-2.

We'd had a lot of visitors. Edgar Snow, author of *Red Star Over China* (which I'd read before coming to the CBI), spent two days with us and I conversed with him at length. Snow was an accredited war correspondent, so I could brief him on our situation. He was also interested in how this Chinese American became a Japanese intelligence specialist.

My trip to New Delhi really paid off as we planned for the Second Burma campaign. In his directive General Boatner said: "You will coordinate all G-2 activities and techniques of this headquarters with our rear echelon, the 10th Air Force, and headquarters of the U.S.

Army Supply Services (SOS) at that place (New Delhi)." I had studied the methods rear echelon and the 10th Air Force used to present tactical situations pictorially and graphically. I had studied their maproom techniques, aerial-photo techniques, and air-mapping systems and discussed G-2 record-keeping, POW interrogation, document translation, and the Japanese unit order of battle, especially that of the Japanese 18th Division in Burma. These observations in New Delhi helped to get us speaking their language at Mile Mark 5 1/2.

No more diaries. That was the directive from Delhi as of 18 April 1943. This would restrict my ability to fully document what went on, but I was certain that with access to official papers, and a good memory for what happens in my part of the world, I would be able to reconstruct pretty well.

At one point General Boatner decided that all of us should become jungle wise and physically fit for combat. We were to train in two-man teams. I was teamed up with Lt. John Kingsbury, our signal officer and my *basha* mate. Fully equipped, we took off at dawn down the jungle trail from Mile Mark 5 1/2 toward Hpachet Hi, twenty-five miles distance. We entered the jungle in just a few hundred yards. It was a different world: the chattering of monkeys in the trees, the hum of thousands of insects, the shrill cry of jungle birds. We were the only humans for miles around. I shall never forget that twenty-four hours. Tall trees, well over 150 feet and more in height, formed a canopy over the jungle through which little light penetrated. Smaller trees, lush jungle vegetation, and meandering streams were our immediate surroundings.

The jungle was full of life. Spiders, of which I was never very fond, predominated. Some were five to six inches in width and I watched in amazement as a group of them attempted to catch a bird in flight! Huge butterflies with wing spans of almost twelve inches fluttered through the trees while thick, shiny, black leeches dropped onto us from tree limbs as we passed beneath. Even the very ground beneath our feet moved as if it were alive. On a closer look, it was. An army of huge ants moved along the trail, carrying dead leaves and insects with them.

The hours passed and without warning darkness closed around us with a suddenness that only occurs in a jungle or a rain forest. We selected a small clearing with a bit of dry ground large enough to spread out our ground cloths. We built a small fire and heated our

C-rations in Kingsbury's steel helmet. Pulling mosquito netting over our heads, we tried to sleep. But sleep wouldn't come. The monkeys continued to howl, the mosquitos buzzed angrily and some found their way through the netting to feast on us. We heard snakes slithering through the underbrush. I burned at least a dozen leeches from my legs and ankles and I suppose Kingsbury did the same. I doubt that either of us slept more than an hour and after what seemed to be an endless night we painfully crawled out of the sacks, heated some powdered coffee, and headed back to Mile Mark 5 1/2. We had learned about the jungle—boy, had we learned. I developed a greater respect for the Chinese Ping and the American GI, who had to exist and fight in this hostile environment day after day, night after night. This trek made me a better intelligence officer, but Kingsbury and I were both thankful to see the bashas of Mile Mark 5 1/2.

I had been playing poker occasionally for relaxation, but one night's experience almost made me give it up. Al Larson, Colonel McNally, Colonel Cannon, Vernon Slater, and I had assembled in Colonel Cannon's basha for a friendly game. Slater went back to his own basha to get some "funny money" (military scrip) before play began. The next thing we heard were loud shouts and cries from the direction of Slater's basha followed by the sound of shots from a 45-caliber pistol. We ran to Slater's basha with our pistols drawn. On the dirt floor, still thrashing, was a sixteen-foot python, its head smoking and bleeding. The poker game finally got underway, but our hearts weren't in it and it broke up early. Everyone checked their bashas and bunks very, very carefully before turning in.

Bashas are native huts favored by those who live in the jungles and hills of north Burma and northeast India. Bamboo poles form the uprights and rafters. The outside walls are made of large bamboo and palm leaves and the insides are made of burlap. The roof is either thatch or, for the more affluent, corrugated iron sheets. The floors are hard-packed dirt. That's all brother. All kinds of animals inhabit the walls and roof thatch. Fiery, biting ants burrow into the dirt floor. The legs of our bunks were placed in cut-off C-ration cans filled with a mixture of oil and water to keep the ants from becoming unwanted bed companions. Large rats, foot-long lizards, and an occasional snake were our constant neighbors. Indian laborers constructed these makeshift quarters and as our staff increased, more and more bashas went up. I saw one Indian worker bitten by a krait, the deadliest of snakes, as he was placing a bamboo pole. He screamed, fell to the ground writhing in pain, and in less than thirty seconds he was dead.

The monsoon months gave us an opportunity to meet many of the Chinese officers. We all got to know Col. Lui Teh-shing, the G-3 of the Chih Hui Pu. He was a graduate of a British military school, spoke English with a decided British accent and was known as Sandhurst Lui. To me, however, Col. Tan Gian-chao, adjutant of the 38th Division was number one. He was fluent in not only English but in Mandarin, Cantonese, French, and Italian, having acquired the latter by graduating from the Italian Military College as an exchange student before the war. He greatly facilitated my trips to units of the 38th Division during the early months of 1944, and armed with his instructions I felt much more comfortable and confident when I approached the perimeter of Chinese frontline units. When he called on General Boatner and Colonel Cannon, he would also drop by to give me an update on what was going on. Colonel Tan and I met again in the early sixties in Washington, D.C. when he was a patient at the Walter Reed Army Hospital and where he often visited my wife's restaurant, the Nanking. He later died at Walter Reed and I was privileged to be a representative of the United States at his funeral.

Planning went on at a hectic pace. I'd been able to make reconnaissance flights over the Hukawng Valley. Since enemy activity in the valley usually occurred near the water or at a bend in the river, we took photos of selected areas near the Tarung and Tanai rivers. If we were fortunate, we spotted occasional activities, sites and trails, from Shingbwiyang to Sharaw Ga and Kantau. This was all enemy territory and we'd been told by natives that there were Burmese units officered by Japanese roaming the area. Because of the dense jungle, we did not see any.

Flying the Hump could be hazardous to your health. One of our C-46s didn't make it on 2 August and its occupants were forced to bail out over the jungle southeast of Ledo. Among them were John P. Davies, General Stilwell's political officer: Eric Severeid and Duncan Lee, both well-known war correspondents, the latter now with the OSS, and a crew of three. Upon getting the word, we immediately notified personnel of the OSS and USAAF who were on the ground, and with the combined efforts of all concerned the downed passengers and crew were brought to safety and taken to Chabua. None suffered more than minor injuries.

Cummings, Colling, and Chan. We were known as the Three Cs at NCAC combat headquarters. Cummings, born of missionary parents in Burma, knew the area, the people, and many of the Hill Tribe languages. Colling was born in Tientsin, China, spoke Mandarin like a Chinese and was used on many sensitive and special projects. To the Three Cs, add Pete Lutken, who could outwalk anybody at the headquarters. We were all specialists in our respective fields.

I still remember my disappointment, however, when one day Colonel Cannon told me that I would remain with the combat headquarters staff and not join the V Force with Cummings, Colling, and Lutken. Later these officers became part of Detachment 101 and still later Colling joined the Dixie Mission to Mao Tse-tung and his Communist forces in Yenan.

The Opium Story

In the hills of north Burma where the borders of the Laos Democratic People's Republic, the Socialist Republic of the Union of Burma, and the Kingdom of Thailand meet today is an area known as the Golden Triangle. It is here that the opium poppy is planted, harvested, and processed for shipping to places such as Marseilles and Istanbul where it is refined into heroin. Eventually it winds up on the streets of the major cities of the world: a multibillion-dollar enterprise. When Mao Tse-tung's Communists defeated Chiang Kai-shek's forces in 1949, units of the Chinese Army known as the Kuomintang (KMT), located in Yunnan Province, fled across the border into neighboring Burma and Laos, eventually penetrating northern Thailand. These organized and armed KMTs took over the lucrative opium trade and, as far as I know, still control it today.

I could have been the opium king of north Burma. Off and on from September 1943 until I left for home in late December 1944, I "controlled" the opium traffic for the Chih Hui Pu. It is not generally known that the United States Army dealt in opium; in fact, I've found no mention of it in any official or, for that matter, unofficial histories of World War II in the China-Burma-India theater of operations. Nevertheless, trade in it we did and in rather sizeable amounts.

It was mid-September 1943. We were at Ledo and I was still assistant to Colonel McNally. In the basha where we worked, the colonel had a standard U.S. Army field safe. He went over to the safe, showed me the combination and handed me a large key. "Open it," he said.

When I swung back the heavy steel door all I could see was a large number of packages. Each package was about three inches by three inches, wrapped in what appeared to be a heavy cheesecloth or burlap and sealed with some kind of a waxy substance. Oh yes, there were some documents in the safe but the colonel ignored them.

"Opium." That's all he said, "opium"—as if it were the most natural thing in the world for a colonel of the United States Army to have a safe full of opium in his office in a native basha in the middle of the jungle!

What did we do with it? Where did we get it? It seems that the British had been using opium as trade goods or in lieu of currency for a long time and had passed that knowledge on to us. We in turn supplied the dark brown, viscous stuff to the Chinese forces, the Marauders, Detachment 101, the V Force and others. They in turn were supposed to use it to pay their native porters, laborers, and, of course, informers. How they distributed the fruit of the poppy I don't know for certain. By my roughest estimates, however, the Allies in India and Burma must have dispensed at least twenty kilos a month for at least twenty-four months of the Second and Third Burma campaigns. That's over a thousand pounds or $240,000!!

Is there a moral to all this? I really don't know. I doubt that we made addicts of any of the Shans, Kachins, or Karens. Most had smoked the stuff since childhood. It was not only expedient to pay for their services in opium, it was downright necessary. I doubt that we, or the Japanese, would have been able to obtain those essential services of portage, labor, or intelligence, if we had not done so. We kept no records of this activity. The SOS apparently retained no records and the British would undoubtedly deny the whole thing. But it did happen. I was there.

PART II
RETURN TO BURMA

First MISLS class at Crissy Field, Presidio of San Francisco, California, January 1942. L to R, Capt. John Burden; Lt. John White; Lt. Lachlan Sinclair (partially hidden); Lt. Roy M. Hirano; Lt. Won-loy Chan; Lt. E. Wright; Capt. Sheldon Covell; Capt. David Swift; Maj. Joseph Dickey; Lt. Gilbert Ayres; Lt. Donald Botting; Lt. Lawrence Dowd; Lt. Robert Pang. (Note: Lt. Dowd was Administrative officer; Lt. Hirano was a member of the administrative staff.)

Capt. Charlie Chan somewhere on the Stilwell Road (that's a road?) January 1944.

Captain Chan and the first Japanese POW taken in the Second Burma campaign. Yupbang Ga, Burma, 24 December 1943.

Col. Joseph W. Stilwell, Jr. and Capt. Won-loy Chan at NCAC Forward Headquarters, Shingbwiyang, Burma, February 1944.

Sgt. Ichimura, unidentified Chinese officer, Capt. Chan, and a Japanese POW. Taihpa Ga, Burma, February 1944.

Dr. (Lt. Col.) Gordon Seagraves and Capt. Won-loy Chan at Taihpa Ga, Burma, 6 March 1944.

Captain Chan, a Japanese POW, GI guard, and Sgt. "Yas" Koike at Shaduzup, Burma, May 1944.

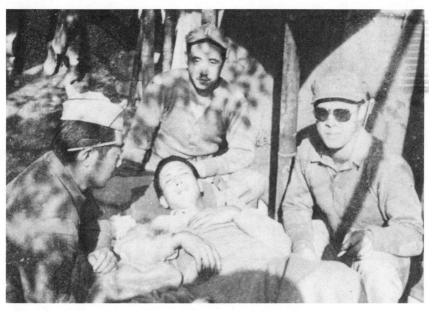

Sgt. Koike, Japanese POW, Sgt. Ichimura, and Capt. Chan. Shaduzup, Burma, May 1944.

Entering the Hukawng Valley

As we moved into October 1943, it became obvious that the Japanese were stepping up their efforts to stop the progress of the Stilwell Road. My work increased. Colonel McNally was away on special assignments nearly all of October. Lt. Patton went back to his own unit leaving me once again the only assigned officer in G-2. The Japanese were conducting delaying actions in the Hukawng Valley and the Taro Plain, but our estimate was that their major defensive effort would center at Jambu Bum, a natural barrier farther south. We knew that our Chinese troops would be up against elements of the Japanese 18th Division, conquerors of Malaya and Singapore, battle tested and tough and now commanded by Gen. Tanaka Shinichi, a seasoned veteran of many campaigns. Faced with the task of breaking through the Japanese defenses was the Chinese 38th Division, relatively untried in combat except during the disastrous First Burma campaign and with the added handicap of Chinese military tradition: defensive rather than offensive operations.

In one of my weekly reports in early October, I stressed the point that the Japanese would probably remain on the defensive in the Kamaing area but would vigorously patrol to the north. These patrols would most likely work the general line of the Tanai and Tarung rivers. Our estimates of Japanese troop strengths in the entire Hukawng Valley area varied from three to four hundred. This bit of intelligence was given to the 38th Division in field orders issued by combat headquarters in early October. With much prodding from General Boatner, the 38th finally moved south from Tagap to Shingbwiyang, then to the Tanai-Tarung area during the last week of October. Here they made contact with the Japanese and the Second Burma campaign, the one to retake Burma, actually began.

It wasn't a very auspicious beginning. After the initial contact, the Chinese, true to their tradition, dug in and nothing General Boatner could say or do could move them. Chinese Gen. Sun Li-jen claimed that his intelligence reported at least a regiment of Japanese facing the 38th. We stuck to our estimate of less than a battalion. Who was right?

After the war we were to learn our estimate had been correct. On 13 January 1948 and again between 25 and 29 April 1949, Gen. Tanaka Shinichi was interrogated by U.S. military intelligence (see Appendix). According to Tanaka only one company, one hundred men with two heavy machine guns, faced elements of the Chinese 38th Division, three thousand men with machine guns, mortars, and artillery support! When the battle was joined on or about 30 October, Tanaka said he ordered the balance of the 2nd Battalion, 56th Regiment, four hundred men with six heavy machine guns, to reinforce the one company. Thus in early November a total of not more than five hundred Japanese with eight heavy machine guns and no artillery or mortars made up the foe that faced Gen. Sun Li-jen. An after-action report stated:

> In the Hukawng Valley, the Chinese 38th Division ran into trouble. . . . The usual mistakes of inexperienced troops were made. Security was inadequate, patrolling almost nonexistent. Early reverses led the troops to dig in deeply and refuse to move. A redeeming feature was the tenacious defensive ability shown. No matter how much the green troops got themselves into trouble never once did they yield an inch of ground that they had taken. However, the division commander lost all desire to attack and his subsequent actions were cautious to the point of timidity.

Tanaka's interrogation, however, would seem to prove that our estimate of enemy strength was the correct one.

The fall of 1943 was rough indeed. With Colonel McNally at the front I was working twenty-four-hour days. Fighting units were yelling for air-photo missions; briefing after briefing became a way of life; additional reports and estimates were ordered by the chief of staff almost daily; enemy documents that filtered back required translation ASAP. I was again the only one at combat headquarters with Japanese-language capability. Added to all that, the enemy was active in our rear areas and G-2 was involved. In the native bazaars, Nepalese and Tibetans listened to speeches that gave accurate information on Gen. Boatner's illness and his being in the base hospital. Possibly as a result, Dinjan was hit by twenty enemy bombers accompanied by twenty-five fighters on 23 December—some Christmas present! I wrote home:

> I feel tired. I've been working hard the past few months and now feel the effects of it. When I overwork and things go wrong I go to a corner by myself, look at the pictures of you people back home and then I feel better—that is what I'm doing now.

Capt. Robert Greene was assigned to G-2 in late November. He was eventually to become my replacement. Gen. Boatner had told me to be ready to move on a moment's notice. It wouldn't take me that long. All my worldly goods, mostly extra clothing and letters from home, were in a small footlocker.

In the middle of all this, on 8 November 1943, I learned that I had been promoted from second lieutenant to captain. Through some administrative foul-up, I never did officially hold the rank of first lieutenant!

With Yasuharu Koike's arrival in December 1943 and Toichi Ichimura's arrival a little later, combat headquarters got its first Japanese American MISLS language team. "Yas" Koike got there in time to interrogate the first Japanese prisoner captured alive on Christmas Eve 1943. (Two Japanese were captured, one died of wounds.) In efforts to get the prisoner to talk he was plied with cigarettes and fried chicken (authorized by General Boatner), which helped. Unfortunately, as the general later said, "The prisoner was too dumb to be of much intelligence value." Because the prisoner was ill we started working out procedures for handling sick and wounded prisoners with the 20th General Hospital as well as with the Office of War Information (OWI) through John K. Emmerson in Margherita. The Chinese Army provided the guards at our combat headquarters in the jungle. With the arrival of Japanese Americans Ichimura and Koike, I had to really impress on the Pings that the two Nisei were on our side—were, in fact, valuable human assets to be protected! It wasn't easy to get this across, believe me.

Many Chinese Americans were in uniform and serving Uncle Sam in faraway places. Those serving in the CBI were mostly in India and China. In October 1943 only five Chinese Americans were listed on our roster as being in Burma. They were Lt. James Chan, QMC, and Capt. Robert Chan, Ord, and myself. Captain Chan came over with me on the *Île de France*. He was from Georgia and spoke Cantonese with a southern accent. Two enlisted men on our roster were Louie D. Fong and Yee J. Lee.

I'm certain we all faced many of the same problems and ran many of the same risks. Like the great majority of Chinese Americans, we spoke the dialect of Canton and had to learn Mandarin in order to converse with our Chinese allies. To many, all Asian Americans looked alike and thus we faced the risk that we all could be, and were, easily mistaken for Japanese. Even our Chinese allies occasionally made this mistake!

On the lighter side of the war, Maj. Stuart Crossman, now my basha mate, accompanied me on my eating trips in and around Ledo. By this time Ledo boasted three Chinese restaurants and in true military fashion, combat headquarters in January 1944 put out a "Memo" on them. In its wisdom the headquarters decided that The New World Cafe and The United Cafe would be authorized for use by enlisted men only. The New Olive Cafe was authorized for use by officers, nurses, and warrant officers only! I suspect there was some crossover.

By mid-December General Stilwell's patience with Gen. Sun Li-jen had run out. Stilwell left the protocol of SEAC, the political machinations of Chungking, and the U.S.-British infighting of New Delhi to take personal command of the Chinese Army in the field. After inspecting frontline units and positions, going over plans with Chinese unit commanders, and talking with Gen. Boatner and his staff, General Stilwell made his decision. He called Gen. Sun Li-jen into his tent. No record of what was said between the two remains but the next day the Chinese began to move!

Asian Americans in the Combat Zone

At the Quebec Conference (Quadrant) in August 1943, Allied planners agreed to a 3,000-man U.S. combat force for General Stilwell in the CBI. Stilwell had had visions of an army corps and hopes for at least a combat division, but he took the Quadrant decision with the philosophical good grace of the professional soldier. By the time of the Cairo Conference (Sextant) in November 1943, the agreed upon combat force was in training in northeastern India, and although its final organization and combat role had not yet been decided upon, it had been patterned along the lines of the British Wingate-led Chindits, Long-Range Penetration Groups (LRPGs) that had penetrated Burma with indifferent success in 1943. The U.S. force was all volunteer. The unit was given the designation 5307 Composite Unit (Provisional). However, with the assignment of Brig. Gen. Frank D. Merrill as the commander, an American newsman christened the unit Merrill's Marauders in his first dispatch from Shingbwiyang in February 1944, and the name stuck.

Retaking Mitch (the GIs name for Myitkyina) was the key to a successful Second Burma campaign as well as the key to the completion of the Stilwell Road to China. To retake not only Myitkyina but also all of north Burma, Stilwell had the Chinese 22nd and 38th divisions that he had reorganized and retrained at Ramgarh; the 5307th, Merrill's Marauders; Wingate's Chindits; the Kachin Levies; some native irregular forces; and for field intelligence, the U.S. Detachment 101. There was also another Chinese division—the 30th—still in training, which on paper at least constituted a reserve. All told, Stilwell's combat effectives numbered about 55,000. Air support consisting of fighters, bombers, and cargo (air drop) was provided by the 10th USAAF. To defend and retain control of north Burma, the Japanese had the 18th Division, now under command of Maj. Gen. Tanaka Shinichi, parts of the 56th and 53rd divisions attached to Tanaka's force, and assorted army and corps units for support. We estimated that Tanaka had between 40,000 and 50,000 battle-tested troops at his disposal. His air support was provided by the Japanese 28th Air Regiment based at Rangoon. To signal the entry of American combat troops into the Second Burma campaign, Merrill's Marauders took off on their first combat mission on 24 February 1944. The mission: cut the Kamaing Road near Walawbum. Meanwhile, the Chinese 22nd and 38th divisions had advanced some sixty miles into the Hukawng Valley against elements of the Japanese 18th.

On orders from Colonel Stilwell, I set out from Ledo for our forward echelon at Shingbwiyang on 30 January 1944. With me was Maj. Fred Eldridge who doubled as General Stilwell's public relations officer and editor of the *CBI Roundup,* our answer to the *Stars and Stripes.* It took us thirty hours of driving over almost nonexistent roads from Ledo to Shingbwiyang. The heavy winter monsoon rains had turned what once might have been a road into a sea of mud in which my trusty jeep Old J-4 got stuck again and again and again. When this happened, Fred and I took turns, one driving and one pushing. We finally pulled into the forward echelon at about 1800 hours on 31 January 1944. Col. Joseph W. Stilwell, Jr., who was to be my new boss, was off on a trip to see his father, General Stilwell, and visit some Chinese troop units near Ningam Sakan. The fight to retake Burma, General Stilwell's Second Burma campaign, was underway. Once again I was the acting G-2 and the combat intelligence officer at the most forward echelon of the combat headquarters.

Intelligence gathering has always been one of the most important activities for any military force. A commander—whether he commands a battalion, division, or army—bases his plans for either attack or defense largely on the information available to him regarding the strengths, weaknesses, weapons, supplies, and morale of the enemy he faces. Intelligence gathering in the CBI and, in particular, in Burma was a difficult task. The enemy spoke and wrote only one language: Japanese, a language written in *kanji* (characters similar to those used in Chinese) that very few persons outside of Japan, unless they were of Japanese origin, spoke, read, or wrote. Only the few Nisei assigned to General Stilwell's headquarters, the Nisei with Merrill's Marauders, and I had this ability. There weren't very many of us and we were all products of the MISLS.

On the Allied side, things weren't much better. The bulk of our forces in the field in direct contact with the Japanese were the Chinese, and the average Chinese Ping had little or no formal education. Most could not read or write, so Japanese kanjis or Chinese kanjis were both Greek to the guy in the line who was most likely to retrieve documents, etc., from the bodies of dead Japanese or collect them from prisoners.

As for prisoners—forget it! In the early days of the Second Burma campaign, we of General Stilwell's intelligence staff rarely saw one. We would get a report that the 2nd Company of the 114th Regiment had taken three prisoners, and we would immediately rush down to the lines by whatever means possible to interrogate them. Usually by the time we got there, we would be greeted by the company commander. "So sorry," he would say. "Prisoners tried to escape and we had to kill them." Repeated efforts by Colonel Stilwell to correct this situation were of no avail and for that matter, neither were the orders sent down by General Stilwell.

This serves to emphasize General Stilwell's biggest problem, actually the biggest problem of any American in dealing with the Chinese. Although General Stilwell, in theory at least, was commander of all Chinese forces in the CBI, or to be more specific, the Burma-India part of that theatre, and was supposed to be able to exercise that command authority through the Chih Hui Pu, in matter of fact he could not. Commanders in the field gave lip service to the Old Man, as they called Stilwell, but they "obeyed" his orders only if parallel orders came down to them through Chinese channels or directly from the Generalissimo himself. As a result, it was not until General Stilwell

convinced Chiang to issue orders regarding the collection of intelligence documents and the retention of prisoners—alive—until they
could be interrogated, that these things came about. From that point
on, 2 March 1944, we got more cooperation from the Chinese units
in the field and were able to give General Stilwell the benefit of it.

Added to the Chinese reporting problem was the problem that
there were not too many Americans who spoke, read, or wrote Chinese.
Except for myself and a few of the "Old China Hands" on Stilwell's
staff, there was no way to determine the accuracy of the translations
of Chinese orders or reports; and the British at least in the beginning
were reluctant to share their intelligence. This problem was corrected
as time went on. The Chinese units weren't our only language problem. There was Detachment 101 with its complement of Kachins who
had no written language. Their reports often had to go through many
hands before they reached us. The data we received now and then
from Brig. Wingate's Chindits weren't much better.

In view of all this confusion regarding the collection, collation,
and evaluation of intelligence, I think it is important to note that Gen.
Tanaka Shinichi confirmed our estimates of Japanese troop strengths
in north Burma in his postwar interrogations.

I finally met my new boss, Col. Joseph W. Stilwell, Jr., on 2
February 1944. He told me that we were now to be known as the
Northern Combat Area Command (NCAC). We discussed the current
situation—that is, he talked and I listened—in some detail. The biggest problem for us in intelligence was, as it has always been, obtaining the raw data, enemy documents, and, of course, prisoners to
interrogate. I'm convinced that the Chinese knew the value of both,
but nevertheless we were not receiving any prisoners and the few
documents that managed to filter back to us were usually out of date
and of little value. While we didn't have positive proof, I suspected
that Japanese prisoners got themselves killed "trying to escape" while
the documents . . . well, there were a lot of uses for paper. In a
letter to the chief of staff in Delhi, General Boatner said in part:

This headquarters is fully aware of the great value of captured
prisoners and documents. Very little of them have been obtained
for the following reasons. The Japanese in this sector, as in all

other sectors, prefer being killed to being captured—taken prisoner. The Chinese, who are our frontline troops, greatly prefer killing them rather than taking them prisoner, because of their experiences in the last six or seven years. Only one Japanese prisoner has been taken. He was badly wounded. He has been courted and pampered by presents and special hospitalization in order to have him talk freely. He's a private and unfortunately too dumb to give us much information. The Chinese are very reluctant to give up captured documents because they themselves have ample facilities for translating them and feel they know more about their value than we do. Nevertheless we put pressure on them and get such documents whenever possible. We have two Japanese translators and one officer trained in Japanese intelligence who then go over the few documents we do receive. In this way the maximum information is obtained with a minimum of delay. After that the documents are sent to your headquarters. So far we have been unable to obtain many of these documents. We do try to obtain them though, and are well aware of their value, and will forward them to you with a minimum of delay.

Getting prisoners and documents from the Chinese was more difficult than pulling teeth!

Colonel Stilwell was pretty unhappy about the whole thing, and pending orders through their chain of command, without which they wouldn't act, he sent me down to the Chinese battalions in the lines hopefully to get at the prisoners and documents before they were killed or lost. He cleared this action with Col. Ni Ying-chung of the 38th Division. My hope was that the clearance would get down to battalion level. As sort of an afterthought, Colonel Stilwell also appointed me the censoring officer for the Seagraves' hospital unit. Since all of Seagraves' nurses were Burmese and I did not speak, read, or write that language, this assignment could have been a problem. Fortunately, they all wrote in English.

After Yasuharu Koike and Toichi Ichimura had arrived at Ledo, they were to come forward to join us. On 5 February Sgt. Toichi "Tom" Ichimura caught an L-5 at Ledo and flew into Shingbwiyang to check out his new home. When Tom climbed out of the L-5 at our little strip, the pilot waved at him and immediately took off. "There was no one in sight. I was all alone," Tom told me later.

My first excursion into the combat zone and no one to meet me. I wandered around the strip for what seemed like hours. Finally a couple of GIs stopped me and after I convinced them that I really was on their side, they told me that they were part of a U.S. advisory group with a Chinese unit. They said that they had some Japanese documents that they had taken from prisoners. They added that the documents were at their command post and asked me if I would go back with them to translate. I agreed and the three of us took off from the strip.

About an hour later we came out of the jungle into a small clearing. Without warning we were surrounded by twenty or twenty-five Chinese soldiers. They were obviously angry and nervous, and all of them had their weapons pointed at me! I couldn't understand their staccato questions in Chinese and I couldn't have answered even if I had. I was pretty certain that this Japanese-American GI was about to meet his Japanese ancestors. Suddenly, from a bunker at the edge of the clearing, an American officer starting yelling at the Chinese—in Chinese! I've got to assume that he explained to the Pings that I was on their side, though from the looks I continued to get, I don't think most of them were convinced.

The officer led me into the bunker, handed me a sheaf of tattered papers, and told me to translate. The bunker was dark and poorly ventilated. The officer gave me the stub of a candle for light. Since I hadn't started out from Ledo to do instant translations, I didn't have pencil or paper and asked the officer for some. He was pretty upset and made some remarks about a stupid translator showing up without the tools of his trade. All he could provide was a roll of toilet paper, the stub of a pencil, and a handful of cooked rice. I glued the toilet paper together with the rice and on the resultant sheets of makeshift paper did the translation. It turned out to be the location of a food dump with the types and amounts of rations it held—out of date, of course. Needless to say, no one was very impressed with me, apparently blaming the translator for the contents of the document! I slept in the bunker that night, but very fitfully and with one eye open.

The next morning I headed back for Shingbwiyang with two other Signal Corps GIs who were headed for their line camp between the Chinese CP and Shing. Since the Japanese had done quite a bit of penetrating in this area, it was a hairy-scary return trip with occasional rifle fire, seemingly directly overhead. I stayed at the line camp and helped the fellas string wire for a couple of days until you [Captain Chan] located me, and I finally got back to the G-2 Section of NCAC at Shingbwiyang.

The Chinese forces had already progressed down the Hukawng Valley and had broken out of the valley to capture the Taro Plain by the end of January 1944. During February, Merrill's Marauders arrived in the Hukawng Valley and Stilwell used them with one Chinese regiment to make a wide sweep east of the road up the valley and to set up a roadblock in the area of Walawbum. The remainder of his forces, with tanks in support, would make a frontal attack on the Japanese at the small town of Maingkwan.

Between 5 and 12 February 1944, Chinese of the 38th Division had advanced to the general line along the north bank of the Tanai River. On the right flank we had cleared the entire Taro Plain and established roadblocks and strong points to prevent enemy access into the area.

On 7 February the 114th Regiment captured four prisoners and sent them to division headquarters. Tom Ichimura and I went to work.

Members of the Japanese language teams were prohibited by Theater Order from going down to Chinese frontline units. It just wasn't safe. The Chinese not only hated the Japanese, the Chinese also didn't seem to be able to differentiate between Japanese and Japanese Americans and were prone to shoot first and ask questions, if any, later. That very same hatred also meant that very few prisoners ever made it to the rear. When the four Japanese taken by the 114th Regiment made it to the 38th Division headquarters, I was sent to interrogate them. Tom Ichimura, in defiance of orders and because, as he said, "there's a job to do," went with me.

The four Japanese turned out to be battle-hardened veterans from the 18th Division, the conquerors of Malaya and Singapore, and they were tough customers. Colonel Ni, G-2 of the 38th Division, had one of his interrogators on hand to observe how the Americans conducted a prisoner interrogation. It was our first frontline interrogation, and I must admit to a certain degree of nervousness. After all, this was not an exercise at the Camp Savage MISLS.

At first the four Japanese refused to say a word. They wouldn't even give us their names and military numbers. With an idea born of desperation, I told Ichimura to translate what I was going to say to each of the four separately—I didn't trust my school-taught Japanese to get across. "Look," I said, with Ichimura giving an almost simultaneous translation, "I'm a captain in the United States Army, but as you can very well see, my skin is the same color as yours. I'm a Chinese American and the sergeant here is a Japanese American. We're trying to get rid of the few samurai Japanese generals and admirals of the Imperial command who deluded the Emperor and got Japan into a war she can never hope to win. We want to get it over with and go home. We want you and the other soldiers like you of whatever nationality to be able to go home also so we can all live in peace. Won't you help us?"

Each of the four looked first at Ichimura and then at me. It was obvious to them that we were of the yellow race. After some moments of indecision they talked. First they made it very clear that they, as soldiers of the Emperor, having been captured, could never go home. Bushido, the Japanese warrior's code, would not permit it. To their families they were dead and would be so reported. We got their names and service numbers as well as their unit designations, and we did obtain some useful order-of-battle information but that was all. They were privates and lance corporals and had very little information of real intelligence value. We never saw them again. The code of Bushido? Probably.

Advance continued on all fronts between 12 and 19 February. We cut the main north-south axis of communications in the Hukawng Valley, the Maingkwan-Taihpa Ga Road, south of Tsumhpawng Ga. The Second Burma campaign was really getting off the ground. The 22nd Division, which had entered the fighting in January, and the 38th Division had been making a steady advance.

Of course, despite what the G-2 and G-3 (operations) periodic reports said, there was really no such thing as a line in this jungle warfare. As Fred Eldridge said, "Both sides deploy forces in what amounts to outposts or strong points which of course permits relatively easy infiltration by either side." But if we were to get any meaningful intelligence, I had to visit so-called frontline units. Leaving the relative safety of NCAC headquarters at Shingbwiyang and visiting the command post of the 38th Division was the first step. Here I would get a briefing by the division G-2 on where he thought the Japanese might be and from the division G-3 on where he thought the Chinese units might be. Fortunately, both of these officers were right most of the time.

It was mid-February when I made my first of what was to be many such forays to Chinese strongpoints and outposts to collect firsthand intelligence. Col. Tan Gian-chao, adjutant of the 38th, was quite concerned about my trips and warned me to be *hsiao hsin* (careful). I tried, although I was painfully aware that dressed in U.S. Army jungle greens and carrying a carbine I must look every inch the Japanese soldier to the usually trigger-happy Chinese Pings that manned the perimeter of the strongpoint. For that matter, I guessed I looked that way to the average American GI, the British Tommy, and our friendly Kachins as well! The only ones I didn't fool were the Japanese. As I approached a perimeter, shots would invariably ring out. I'd hit the ground and in my best Mandarin Chinese yell, "*Pu yao k'ai chiang*" (Don't shoot). After what seemed an eternity, a Ping would yell back, "*Chan chu*" (Stop). Hell, I'd already stopped. This was usually followed by "*Pu yao tung*" (Don't move). I didn't intend to move, although I was shaking like a leaf and feared even that little movement might prove fatal. There would be another interminable wait until a voice said "*K'uo lai*" (Come here). With my hands holding the carbine high above my head and my heart literally in my mouth, I would obey, walking slowly and carefully toward the perimeter until hidden Chinese soldiers seemingly appeared out of nowhere and surrounded me. They escorted me into the perimeter, where I was interrogated by Chinese officers at length until they satisfied themselves that I was a Chinese and not one of the hated enemy.

I didn't find many Pings with whom I could converse in Cantonese, but I shared many a simple meal with small groups of them, doing the best I could with my recently acquired Mandarin. They were simple men, cheerful and at all times courteous. They marveled that, at almost thirty, I was a captain in the U.S. Army but had no wife and no children. Gathering in groups of ten or so, the Pings boiled their rice in large pots, adding chopped vegetables and either meat or fish and that was that. The following day the rice would be eaten cold or reheated, or they would add water and make it into soup. They drank only boiled water, or a rare issue of tea, and seemed singularly free of dysentery.

Despite our efforts, Ichimura, Koike, and I were just not getting the cooperation we needed from the Chinese. As a result we were not getting the kind of intelligence information both General and Colonel Stilwell wanted and needed. Why? The Chinese units—companies, battalions, even regiments—had not been ordered to cooperate with us. Like soldiers the world over, the Chinese were suspicious of outsiders, and unless they received specific orders through their chain of command, they just were not going to cooperate. True, General Stilwell had been designated the Commander-in-Chief of all Chinese forces in India-Burma by no less an authority than the Generalissimo himself, but between the General and the Chinese units in the field were a myriad of intermediate headquarters all commanded and staffed exclusively by Chinese, and they had to receive and pass on the word, even from the Chih Hui Pu. This bit of counterintelligence, if you will, finally got through on our side and in March 1944, all field orders had an intelligence annex attached, authenticated in Chinese, that established channels for prisoner and documents flow. Intelligence collecting improved after that and our trips to the field were fewer.

Many and diversified military, quasimilitary, paramilitary, and other units made up the CBI, probably the most unusual theater of operations during World War II. Two of these stand out in my mind: Detachment 101 of the Office of Strategic Services (OSS) and the 5307 Composite Unit (Provisional), which gained fame as Merrill's Marauders. Detachment 101 operations included espionage, sabotage, and intelligence collection. Maj. Chester Chartrand was assigned as Detachment 101 liaison officer to NCAC. Detachment 101 personnel performed outstanding service in the CBI. Operating behind Japanese lines either as loners or with native Kachins, they risked their lives daily to provide General Stilwell with the intelligence he so urgently needed throughout the Burma campaigns.

Lt. Gen. W. Ray Peers who, as a lieutenant colonel, commanded Detachment 101 from 17 December 1943 until 12 July 1945, culminated his distinguished army career with his investigation of the My Lai incident in Viet Nam. His official report, as well as his published personal account of that incident provided outstanding examples of what an officer and a gentleman should be.

Merrill's Marauders provided its share of outstanding Japanese American (Nisei) and American heroes also.

Between 10 and 26 February our advance continued with only minimal resistance. Right-flank units had rejoined the main body, which now had a front from Lanem Ga, west of Nhkang-Kayang, south to the Tabawng River opposite Makaw.

By February 1944 the Second Burma campaign was well underway. Merrill's Marauders jumped off from Ningbyen with the mission of enveloping the Japanese at Walawbum and linking up with elements of the Chinese 22nd and 38th divisions who were driving the Japanese south-southeast through the Hukawng Valley along the axis of the Taihpa Ga-Maingkwan Road. Forward headquarters of the Chih Hui Pu closed out at Shingbwiyang and opened at Taihpa Ga on February 25. NCAC did the same.

With the 66th Regiment of the Chinese 22nd Division spearheading the advance on the right and the Marauders on the left, General Stilwell hoped to encircle a large portion of the Japanese 18th Division in Hukawng Valley by establishing a series of roadblocks near Walawbum that would allow the remaining five regiments of the 22nd and 38th divisions and Col. Rothwell Brown's Chinese tank force to drive the Japanese into a corner.

On 26 February 1944 our NCAC headquarters set up in a small clearing at Taihpa Ga near the banks of the Tanai Hka (River). We cut a small airstrip in the jungle, just long enough and wide enough to take the L-1, L-4, and L-5 liaison aircraft that kept us in contact with the base at Ledo and provided medical evacuation. We lived in bashas, hastily thrown together, usually from wood (teak!), bamboo, and rushes. We worked out of British double-walled army field tents.

Our intelligence staff was growing. In addition to Col. Stilwell and myself, there was Lt. Erle Stewart, S. Sgt. Bert Weiner, and Pfc Carl Tarlpinian; Sgts. Tom Ichimura and "Yas" Koike of the language team, plus Capts. Schmelzer and Robbins, who operated the recently acquired photo intelligence unit. The U.S. liaison officers to the Chinese 22nd and 38th divisions dropped by our shop frequently to get the latest enemy information. I got the impression that their Chinese counterparts didn't tell them very much.

Jade!

Burma used to provide the women of the world with some of its most precious stones. The ruby mines of Burma near Mandalay were world famous, and you can bet that the British didn't want the American GIs or the Chinese Pings anywhere near them. When the boundaries were drawn between General Slim's XIV British Army and General Stilwell's combat forces of the NCAC and the Chinese Army in India, Admiral Mountbatten made certain that all the rubies were in Slim's area!

Jade, on the other hand, was to be found in north Burma in large quantities. The area adjacent to the trace of the Stilwell Road and the upper reaches of the Hukawng Valley from the India-Burma border along the Wantuk Bum down to the Ahawk Hka had a number of active mines still operating. Chinese troops of the 22nd and 38th divisions were not long in discovering this fact. Nor did it take them long to find out that local mine superintendents were not loath to part with their precious wares in return for promises of protection for themselves, their workers, and their property. The owners of the mines fled when the Japanese came in, so the mine supervisors figured they were in charge.

It didn't take long either for some of our more enterprising American officers serving as advisors (liaison) with Chinese units to see the possibilities for making a quick fortune.

An officer came into my tent at Shaduzup one afternoon in late May 1944. He looked around to make certain we were alone. "Charlie," he said in almost a stage whisper, "I've got something to show you." He was carrying an olive-drab rubberized ration bag about the size of a small grocery sack. He untied the string, turned it upside down, and onto my desk fell chunks of what appeared to be rough gray stones. There were about ten of them ranging in size from a golf ball to a tennis ball and about fifty others, rough cut but in a myriad of colors—green, oxblood, black, and red—ranging in size from a large marble to a Ping-Pong ball. "Know what these are?" asked the officer. I admitted that I did not. Taking a GI trench knife from his belt, he proceeded to gouge into one of the rough gray stones. As the outer crust peeled away the stone turned a beautiful dark green. "Jade, Charlie," he said. "All of these are jade, the reds, the blacks, all of 'em." He had convinced one of the mine supervisors that he controlled the Chinese troops in the area and could assure full protection to the supervisor, his mine, and his workers. The officer seemed proud of what he had done although he knew that I knew that he couldn't actually control any of the Chinese and that he couldn't very well protect anyone either.

"You're staff, Charlie," he said. "You've got to have a way to get this back to the states. What'll you give me for the lot." I didn't want to get involved in this nefarious business, but neither did I wish to offend the officer or make him my enemy. I had priced, polished and finished jade in Ledo and in New Delhi. Even a rough calculation by weight told me that this sackful must be worth at least $10,000. "I'd sure like to help you," I said. "How about $1,000?"

"Come on, Charlie," he answered. "It's got to be worth at least $5,000." I explained that even if I agreed with him, which I did not, I didn't have that much money on hand. In fact, I only had $800 and would have to borrow the rest.

The officer shrugged his shoulders, put his rocks back in the sack, and left. I never did learn what he did with the jade, but if he eventually got it back to the states and hung onto it, it would be worth about $500,000 today. I guess I just wasn't cut out for a life of crime—any kind of crime. If I had been I could have been an opium king or a jade smuggler. Instead, I'm a retired army officer. As it was, when I left Burma and the CBI for the last time, I took with me a single piece of jade purchased in New Delhi for 300 rupees ($100.00). My wife still has it.

Hukawng to Mogaung—Imphal

The first part of Stilwell's Second Burma campaign went well. By mid-March 1944 all organized Japanese resistance in the Hukawng Valley had ceased. We estimated over 2,000 Japanese had been killed. Large amounts of supplies including hundreds of thousands of rounds of ammunition from small arms to 150-mm shells, vehicles, weapons, and even elephants were among the booty. Over 250 square miles had been occupied with more than forty Burmese villages liberated.

The Chinese 38th and 22nd divisions swept down the Kamaing Road axis, took Maingkwan, and moved on toward Walawbum. Meanwhile, the Marauders moved down the eastern flank of the Hukawng Valley in a series of well-executed moves to establish roadblocks in the vicinity of Walawbum and the Nambyu Hka crossings northeast of the town. Elements of the Chinese 38th Division closed on Walawbum on 7 March. Typical of incidents when Asian and Caucasian troops represent both ally and enemy, the Chinese fired on the Marauders who were manning the roadblocks and the Marauders fired back, seriously wounding four Chinese before recognition was finally established.

By 11 March 1944 we had closed out at Taihpa Ga and opened NCAC forward headquarters at Maingkwan about ten miles north of Walawbum along the Kamaing Road. Merrill's Marauders were just a few miles away in bivouac preparing for their next mission and at the same time getting a bit of well-deserved rest. In reading a periodic report of their last action, a few sentences caught my eye. "On 6 March, Walawbum was isolated. Six Japanese officers and eighty men were killed. A Japanese telephone line was tapped; messages were intercepted and interpreted. Japanese appeals for help and reinforcements got immediate response from us. On 9 March 1944 we intercepted an order from the 18th Division for the Japanese to retreat. We caught them in their assembly area."

The only way that the Americans could translate the Japanese intercepts was by using a Japanese American classmate of mine from Camp Savage who had volunteered for hazardous duty with the Marauders. I learned later that S. Sgt. Roy Matsumoto had done the wire-tap and most of the translations.

By 18 March our troops were at the entrance to the Moguang-Kamaing Valley. In less than five months the NCAC's Chinese and American troops had advanced about 100 miles on a 75-mile front. This latest offensive, which carried itself to the Jambu Bum area, fascinated me because in late 1943 I had made a detailed topographical study of the area. G-2 figured that the Japanese would stage a series of delaying actions there. We took the Jambu Bum ridge with the 66th Regiment on 18 March. The Japanese counterattacked on 19 March and again the Chinese drove them back. With the occupation of the Jambu Bum the NCAC headquarters moved from Maingkwan to Tingkawk Sakan and on 22 March I climbed the Jambu Bum to get a firsthand look at what the Japanese Army had tried so hard to defend.

Now that the first phase of the Second Burma campaign had been successfully concluded, our supreme commander in Southeast Asia, Admiral Mountbatten, paid us a visit. I suspect he came to NCAC headquarters to confer with General Stilwell. What a contrast these two professional military men presented. Lord Louis, related to the British royal family, was the prototype of the British aristocrat. Tall, handsome, perhaps in his forties, he wore the beautifully pressed, tropical worsted suntan uniform of a full admiral in the Royal Navy complete with rows of ribbons. Around his trim waist was a tan web belt from which was suspended a tan web pistol holster with the butt of what appeared a Webley showing. Tan web gaiters, looking like spats, covered the tops of highly polished tan shoes, and on his head was a tan billed cap with enough "scrambled eggs" on the patent leather visor to make a respectable omelet.

General Stilwell was the prototype of the middle-class American. Of medium height, skinny, craggy of feature, wearing steel-rimmed GI spectacles, he looked every one of his sixty years, and resembled a country schoolteacher more than he did the commander of thousands of Chinese and American troops. He wore baggy green GI pants tucked into old-fashioned canvas leggin's and a much-washed khaki shirt under an unpressed khaki field jacket. On his head, in place of his usual battered Army campaign hat, was a Chinese army forage cap. He showed no insignia of rank, wore no ribbons, and carried no weapons, not even a general's pistol.

We turned out the entire NCAC staff, including a contingent of Doctor Seagraves' Burmese nurses, who looked mighty pretty in their best longyis and spotless white shirtwaists. The rest of us, in jungle-green fatigues or unpressed khakis, didn't look too impressive. The general introduced, or rather presented, us to the admiral who spoke briefly on what an outstanding job we were performing. I noticed that his eyes were on the Burmese girls as he spoke. The two commanders then climbed into the jeep and took off quickly. General Stilwell didn't speak to us but he wasn't known to hand out compliments very often.

The next advance after the capture of Walawbum was down the line on the road to Kamaing. General Stilwell made a frontal attack down the road with his Chinese divisions supported by tanks, while the Marauders split into two columns and went off on a wide sweep to the east through very difficult country, aiming to cut back and establish roadblocks at Shaduzup, and again ten miles farther south at Inkangahtawng. The OSS Kachin irregulars gave a valuable screen to this operation. The Japanese reacted swiftly and vigorously and immediately sent a force of more than three battalions up from Kamaing to remove the block. After days of fierce fighting, the Japanese withdrew leaving the Americans and Chinese holding the area.

Possibly because of the setbacks they were suffering in north Burma in mid-March, the Japanese stepped up their campaign against the British XIV Army on the India-Burma border near Imphal and the Assam-Bengal Railway. Lt. Gen. Renya Mutaguchi, commanding the Japanese 15th Army in Burma, had long wanted to do this as a preemptive strike, but the British did not believe that the Japanese could move so fast over such difficult terrain. I guess the lessons of Malaya and Singapore hadn't gotten into the British military textbooks yet.

General Mutaguchi's forces struck hard. In the face of our overwhelming air superiority and misreading (perhaps intentionally) the natural environment and the magnitude as well as the mobility of General Slim's XIV Army, Mutaguchi attempted a three-pronged assault, a veritable blitzkrieg against Imphal. Intent on a quick, decisive victory that would open the door to India, General Mutaguchi launched his three combat divisions—the 15th, 31st, and 33rd—on three separate routes toward Manipur over rugged, mountainous country fronted by the formidable barrier of the Chindwin River. He gave the divisions twenty days' rations along with the bare minimum of ammunition. Their orders were obviously succeed or die.

To defend India from this invasion (although Tanaka Shinichi during his post-war interrogation said that the Japanese never had any intention of going beyond the Burma-India border and cutting the Assam-Bengal Railway), Gen. William Slim had the British XIV Army, consisting of four army corps with a total of nine divisions one of which had five Long Range Penetration Groups (LRPGs) known as the Chindits. They had taken this name from the mythological Burmese *chinthe*, half-lion, half-bird, that protects Burmese temples. Each group was roughly brigade size with the total Chindit strength being about 12,000 officers and men. They were commanded by Brig. Orde Wingate, a bearded Britisher cut from the cloth of Lawrence of Arabia. He had led the first Chindits (about 3,000 men) into Burma from India in early 1943, and they had penetrated in small groups for about 200 miles into north and north central Burma. Less than two thirds of the force got back to India alive.

Nevertheless, Wingate, a charismatic character who deeply impressed Churchill, persuaded the British high command to give him four times the number of the original force to try again. At the same time his theory of long range penetration was adopted as a model for Merrill's Marauders, initially over strenuous objections from General Stilwell. For this effort, however, Wingate was in much better shape and really had an objective. Four of his five LRPGs (10,000 men) were flown into Burma by glider. In fact Wingate even got his own air force, the 1st Air Commando, consisting of C-47s, Waco CG4A gliders, a squadron of P-51 fighters, a squadron of B-25 bombers, and numerous L-series aircraft for communication and evacuation of wounded. This heterogeneous group was commanded by Col. Philip Cochrane, USAAF, who was to be immortalized as Flip Corkin in the comic strip "Terry and the Pirates."

The stage was set for the next phase of Stilwell's Second Burma campaign, although there were still the old problems of split command. Stilwell had his (new) Chinese First Army, Merrill's Marauders, and some assorted U.S. Army units of engineers, signals, and medics. Wingate's Chindits were under Slim's command as was Col. Cochrane's 1st Air Commando, although it was later released to Stilwell. General Stilwell also had Detachment 101, the Kachin Levies, and later some British antiaircraft units.

Lt. Gen. Mutaguchi thrusted through Imphal toward India everything he had and that was considerable. What was his objective? Actually to invade India or just to cut the Assam-Bengal Railway and push the British back into India? We had to try to find out the who, what, where, when, and how for Gen. Stilwell. Reports from our liaison officers with the XIV Army and the intelligence gathered by the Peers Force helped to clear the picture. We knew that Mutaguchi was using his 15th, 31st, and 33rd divisions at Imphal. That apparently left only the 18th Division in north Burma with the 114th Regiment defending the Myitkyina area and elements of the 55th and 56th regiments still in the Hukawng Valley. The Japanese 56th Division, we believed, was still in the Mangshih area, although we had reports that at least one of its regiments had been seconded to Tanaka's 18th Division. How would the Japanese react to being vertically-enveloped by Wingate's Chindits at "Broadway," "Piccadilly," and "Aberdeen," all landing zones (see map) behind the 18th Division? Would the 114th Regiment continue to defend the Myitkyina area or would it move against the Wingate Chindits? The answers would affect General Stilwell's strategy in north Burma.

With the Marauders on the left flank and the Chinese on the right, our forces had moved steadily down the Hukawng Valley toward Walawbum. It was the first time we'd been so close on the heels of the combat units. Set up in tents with foxholes all about, we could hear the sound of battle to our front and flanks.

POWs, Papers, and Psywar

After Chiang Kai-shek's order to Chinese unit commanders, intelligence reports, captured documents, and prisoners came to us with some regularity. Reports from Chinese divisions in the field showed much improvement. The original still went by telegram to the G-Mo daily, but we got a copy to be translated into English for General Stilwell and his staff. I was impressed with the newfound quality of their reports:

> Hq. 38th Div., Weekly Combat Report, Summary, 112th Regiment.
> At 1600 hours 9th Co., 3rd Bn discovered a Japanese Intelligence Center where about 20 enemy soldiers were working. Recon Squad made a surprise attack killing 10 and wounding 5. The balance escaped. Captured 7 weapons, 2 radios, and 3 sets of intelligence orders from a Gen. Aida. Map accompanying the orders showed we are opposed by the 114th Regiment of the 18th Division. West of the road is the 56th Regiment and east of the road is the 55th Regiment. Other documents taken proved that the 114th Regiment is in front of us.

This was a real improvement over reports from Chinese units six months earlier!

Colonel Chiang of General Stilwell's personnel staff consolidated all the reports—no small task—and telegrammed them to Chiang Kai-shek. At the same time a copy went to General Stilwell's headquarters, where his adjutant general made up a Chinese file. Major Lin and others from his translation section worked their butts off to complete translations in time to be of some use to Stilwell's staff. My responsibility for these translated reports was making a daily trek through the mud to get the dope hot off the wire. I'd flag anything I thought would be of special interest to Colonel Stilwell. Nearly every day these translations came in—of the telegrams sent to the G-Mo with copies to General Ho and General Shao of G-Mo's super-high staff. Although Col. Chiang wrote the telegrams they were signed by General Stilwell as the G-Mo's commander in India-Burma.

Of course we continued to receive reports from the G-2s of the two Chinese divisions. Some of these reports were voluminous and of little value, but each had to be laboriously translated just in case it contained some pearl of wisdom. We found it necessary to require our Chinese translators—when converting kanjis to English for proper names—to include the original kanjis or else "Captain Yamamoto" would come out "Captain San Hon" since both Chinese and Japanese use the kanjis. By referring to the original kanjis, our MISLS-trained translators could make the proper conversion to English.

Vitally important to the success of our campaign was the order of battle of the Japanese forces in Burma. I'd started keeping an order of battle notebook in April of 1943—an important step. As the campaign progressed, it became routine for Colonel Stilwell to hold order-of-battle sessions with me and Erle Stewart on an almost daily basis. What Japanese unit is directly in front of us now? In what strength? How can you be certain a company of the 2nd Battalion, 55th Japanese Regiment is on that high ridge at this time? We got him the answers as best we could. Many of them came from or were confirmed by American liaison officers with the Chinese troops who regularly and faithfully reported to NCAC headquarters. We also got a lot of help from the recon and photo missions flown by our small L-4 and L-5 planes, and thanks to a recent order from General Stilwell, these missions were now coordinated by our headquarters and not flown willy-nilly at the order and whim of any subordinate commander.

One of our best sources of intelligence was the flow of documents and POWs from the frontline units. Through his liaison officers, Stilwell conveyed orders that all Chinese units in the field would report by the fastest means available identification of enemy units, condition of enemy uniforms, direction of enemy movements, and enemy locations, including time and date of siting. All captured documents, identification discs, insignia, sleeve patches, and diaries were to be sent to us immediately as were all POWs, except those too badly wounded or too ill to travel, who were evacuated to the nearest field hospital. We didn't get everything. The Chinese Ping is no different from the American GI when it comes to collecting souvenirs and I suspect many a home in the hinterlands of China or in Taiwan has the unit flag from a Japanese regiment, a shoulder patch, an officer's samurai sword, or some other bit of memorabilia hidden away in a chest or displayed on a wall. Nevertheless, we got enough to round out our order of battle (which later events proved to be reasonably accurate).

Incidentally, psychological warfare was not limited to us Westerners. The Japanese had been using it against the Chinese in north Burma. One method that I saw recently was in the form of a leaflet obtained from an officer in the Chinese 38th Division. Written in Chinese, it was about a Chinese hero named Lin Tse-hsu who fought against the British during the Opium Wars and became a national hero. This translation is pretty rough, but I'm going to set it down as we got it:

Mr. Lin Tse-hsu

Do you know this man? Suppose you don't know him, go ask your squad leader; if he still doesn't know, go and ask your platoon leader from whom you will get it. For what has Mr. Lin become so famous? Why could he make all Chinese happy? Think it over. Now, you may compare which is more worthwhile to fight for; the cause of this war or that of the war [that] should be.

Hundred years ago the British sent lots of poisonous opium to China and then took Hong Kong away. Recently, the "big nose" westerners behind you, though support you might rob something from you. Do you know what they want?

Your ancient China is now at stake. You are still unconscious of the cruel means of those "big nose"? Alas: PRETTY

BRUTAL! PRETTY BRUTAL! Hulloh! Turn back quickly! The enemy stand just behind you. Isn't there any Mr. Lin's grandson in your army? Slaughter some of those "big nose." It is no hard task.

As far as I know, no Chinese Ping was enticed to cross over as a result of this crude bit of psywar, nor was any American or British soldier killed as a result either. But come to think of it, I don't recall that any of our more sophisticated "psywar" had any greater effect on the Japanese!

General Stilwell's thrust down the Hukawng Valley with two Chinese divisions and the Marauders and the glider assault by Wingate's Chindits were all going well. But General Slim was having problems on the Imphal front. Mutaguchi's five divisions, relatively unencumbered, moved fast and were able to cut the Imphal-Kohima Road some forty miles inside the Province of Manipur in India. Although we didn't know it at the time, that was to be the high-water mark of the Japanese offensive at Imphal. General Mutaguchi had gambled and lost. India was never again threatened by the Japanese. When the British eventually lost that part of the Empire, it was through politics, not military action.

In looking over my notes, I see that I referred to Gen. Renya Mutaguchi as a reckless, ambitious general. In retrospect, I may have overreacted. Ambitious he was, but I'm not so certain he was reckless—with a little bit of luck his Imphal gamble might have paid off. Mutaguchi was well known to General Stilwell. During the Sino-Japanese War when Imperialist Japan was trying to take over North China, General Stilwell (then a colonel) was the military attache at the American embassy in Peking. About twelve miles west of Peking on the Peking-Hankow Road is a bridge crossing the Yongding River. In Chinese it is called the Lukouchiao, but Westerners know it as the Marco Polo Bridge. It was on this bridge, on 7 July 1937, that Japanese troops fired on Chinese troops, starting the Sino-Japanese War. Commanding the Japanese force was Col. Renya Mutaguchi who, during the planning for the Imphal offensive, is reported to have said that he fired the first shot of World War II at the Marco Polo Bridge and felt that he had to settle the war at Imphal. As a major general,

Mutaguchi commanded the Japanese 18th Division that was instrumental in running General Stilwell and his Chinese forces out of Burma in 1942 and he still headed the 18th in March 1943 when it drove north of Shingbwiyang to Tagap before being checked by elements of the Chinese 38th Division. Mutaguchi took over the Japanese 15th Army in March 1943.

Much has been written about General Joseph W. (Vinegar Joe) Stilwell. He was approaching his sixtieth year when World War II caught up with the United States at Pearl Harbor and he was sent to Asia to command Chinese forces. In Burma General Stilwell lived like the rest of us. His tent or basha was no better than ours. He took his place in the chow line and ate his C-rations with the rest of us. Gourmet food it wasn't and a great part of the time it wasn't even appetizing, but I never heard him complain.

On 19 March 1944 General Stilwell celebrated his sixty-first birthday. I was not at the command post that day but a week later I saw an article by an unknown writer in the *CBI Roundup* which deserves to be quoted:

Sitting in a damp tent surrounded by mud and the jungle, Lt. Gen. Stilwell celebrated his 61st birthday by proceeding with the two things most important to him in this world—killing Japs and reopening communications with China. On his birthday he ate C-rations with his staff although the cooks did come up with a cake for the occasion. After the meal, he returned to his tent to figure out ways and means to reach his next objective now that his Chinese and American troops were wiping out the enemy at Jambu Bum, thus clearing the Hukawng Valley. In his spare time he would memorize queer Burmese names for the towns, villages, roads and rivers of Burma, the various mileages that needed to be covered; he would study drawings he had made in his notebook to illustrate engagements past and planned. He smoked innumerable cigarettes, cursed the weather, and wished for a hot bath—any kind of a bath for that matter. Someday when this war is only a filthy memory, the whole story of Stilwell in Asia will be told. It will be an epic and will be the story of how a skinny, unpretentious, homely little man went forth with sword and slew the dragons in their dens.

In my opinion, General Stilwell could have gone down in American military history with Eisenhower, MacArthur, and Bradley had he been given the field command he so wanted. Instead, he was plunged into the politico-military arena known as the China-Burma-India theater and wound up relieved of his command, sacrificed to expediency.

The Japanese thrust toward Imphal, coupled with Wingate's Chindit landings in the triangle formed by Moguang, Katha and Bhamo, caused the Japanese to change their remaining troop dispositions, and thanks to intelligence gathered by Detachment 101 and documents captured by the Chinese units, we were able to determine what these were and thus get some of the answers General Stilwell and Colonel Stilwell both wanted. We found that elements of the 114th Regiment of the 18th Division, that were supposed to be the defense of Myitkyina, were as far southwest as Mawlu, about 100 miles from Mitch. The Chinese also captured a lieutenant from the 114th who had a lot more to say than just giving his name, rank, and service number. He told us that three companies, the 7th, 8th, and 9th of the 114th (the 3rd Battalion) were at Mawlu. This force was supposed to move north toward Mogaung in an effort to remove the threat that the Chindits posed to Tanaka's base at Myitkyina. From documents the Chinese units sent back to us we also confirmed that elements of the Japanese 56th Division had been seconded to Tanaka and were in the vicinity of Mogaung and Kamaing. It was obvious that the glider assault of the Chindits, coupled with the drive down the Hukawng by the Chinese and the concurrent flanking movement by the Marauders, had the Japanese running around like chickens with their heads cut off.

Our G-2 situation maps became out of date almost as fast as they were posted, and the order-of-battle discussions became hotter and livelier as the days wore on. With only three Japanese linguists on the staff—Yas Koike, Tom Ichimura, and myself—and with more and more captured documents coming in as our troops advanced, the entire G-2 section had been working around the clock to keep up.

On the other hand, there was that so-called funny incident. Yas and Tom scouted around after we moved into Tingkawk Sakan and found a Japanese supply dump that had been abandoned when the Japanese retreated. The dump was in a cave and bats flew out as Yas and Tom went in. They found a good-sized cache of food, gathered what they could, and brought it back and gave it to the Japanese prisoners who were being held in a small compound near the command post. The prisoners were most grateful and putting the whole mess in a big stew pot they cooked it up for a few hours and then invited Yas and Tom to partake of the feast. Yas and Tom had brought their own mess kits and the Japanese prisoner-cook ladled the first scoop into Tom's kit with a great flourish. Tom bowed, took a big mouthful, and damn near gagged as he bit into a king-sized Burmese June bug! Amid much laughter, the Japanese insisted that the bug must have accidently flown into the stew while it was cooking, but Yas and Tom had their doubts. Anyway, Tom was spitting bug legs, wings, and antennas for two days!

We moved twenty miles into the Mogaung-Kamaing Valley, killing at least 700 enemy on the way, between 25 March and 1 April. The Marauders held the left flank, preventing Japanese infiltration, and at their Inkangatawng roadblock, the Marauders killed some 150 enemy who had tried to force the block. By 1 April the Marauders controlled all the trails in the Nhpum Ga-Hsamshingyang area.

Between 1 and 8 April, we traveled the Shaduzup-Kamaing Road axis advancing four miles on a twelve-mile front. From 28 March to 7 April, the 2nd Battalion of the Marauders was cut off and surrounded by Japanese forces at Nhpum Ga for almost two weeks of intensive and bloody fighting. The Marauder 3rd Bn. was having its own problems so the Marauder 1st Bn. finally broke through and relieved the 2nd. It was the first big engagement for Merrill's GIs and they acquitted themselves well. More than 400 enemy were killed, unknown numbers wounded. The Marauders lost fifty-seven killed, 302 wounded.

Around 1 April it was obvious that the British XIV Army was in trouble at Imphal. Japanese columns were around Kohima and had been sighted along the Imphal-Kohima-Dimapur Road only about thirty miles from the Bengal and Assam Railroad, which if cut would imperil the entire supply route from the port of Calcutta to the railhead at Ledo. General Stilwell was concerned with this turn of events and in conference with Lord Mountbatten and General Slim at Jorhat on 3 April he agreed to be responsible for a defense line from Tinsukia (slightly northwest of Ledo) to Nazira (southeast of Ledo), with a strong defense point at Jorhat. He formed the Gasper Force from elements of the 30th Chinese Division, a battalion from Colonel Rothwell Brown's Provisional Tank Group, and a heavy mortar battalion, also from Ramgarh. The Japanese attack, however, petered out and the Gasper Force never got a taste of combat.

Mogaung to Myitkyina

Chinese 38th and 22nd divisions made local advances between 8 and 15 April. The Marauders stopped the Japanese in the hills east of the Mogaung River. The Chinese 30th Division regrouped as we got set to carry out the next mission.

We advanced eight miles into the Mogaung-Kamaing Valley with our front line extending from Nhpum Ga past Auche, Warong, and Manpin to one mile north of Tigrawnyang, generally along the north bank of the Lahkraw River. Regrouping of the 30th continued while the Marauders secured the left flank.

Having broken into the Mogaung Valley by the end of April, Stilwell hoped to advance more rapidly with the 22nd and 38th divisions toward Kamaing and Mogaung and to send the Galahad Force on a wide flanking march to make a surprise attack on Myitkyina.

During March and April of 1944 our command post moved five times: our forces cleared the Hukawng Valley and made ready for the final assault on the main Japanese position at Myitkyina. The frequency of our moves put pressure on our small G-2 section and certainly didn't leave us time to turn out fancy formats or reports such as we had been taught at school and received from New Delhi and from SEAC in Ceylon. We had only one typewriter to get out our G-2 roundups, situations reports, translation series, and POW interrogation reports as best we could. We worked nights to get out the reports on captured documents that were of greatest value to General Stilwell and his staff. We often had to keep the Japanese prisoners with us when we moved and do their interrogations when we could. Most were low ranking, privates or junior NCOs, and we quickly learned that they didn't have much to offer. If by chance we did get a ranking NCO or officer, we went all out. After a couple of scary incidents, we finally got an American MP assigned to us full time to act as a prisoner escort and guard. He took the prisoners to and from the stockade for the interrogations. It seemed that most of the captured documents had a bad habit of arriving in the dead of night, so I'd have to wake Tom and Yas, who would then work through the balance of the night so that Col. Stilwell could have the results on his desk first thing in the morning. These two Japanese Americans and I did our best to keep the order-of-battle file up to date, although this became more difficult as Japanese casualties mounted. It became, as Yas said, "almost impossible to keep up with the changes in company commanders." Then too, the Japanese were forming new units called independent mixed brigades or composite battalions, and it was very difficult to know which units were disbanded and which reorganized to make up such units—but we tried.

Despite Chiang Kai-shek's orders, we still had occasional problems in obtaining prisoners for interrogation. On 9 April, a battalion of the Chinese 65th Regiment took over the village of Wakawng and reported finding fifty-four dead enemy and capturing four prisoners. Unfortunately, the Chinese commander reported, two of the four committed suicide. Bushido again?

At long last we finally got two more MISLS-trained Japanese linguists from New Delhi. Henry Kuwabara and Joe Inafuku joined us in early April. From a G-2 standpoint, their arrival was indeed noteworthy. It allowed us to cope with the vastly increased work load brought about by the influx of enemy documents and additional prisoners. We could now prepare typewritten "mats" of our translation series and interrogation series and thus were able to disseminate them outside our immediate chain of command. By 31 May 1944, wider distribution of the former began while that of the latter soon followed. Without the help of these two Nisei, it couldn't have been done. Henry Kuwabara was soon transferred to the British 36th Division in the Railroad Corridor. Later many additional Japanese American MISLS graduates served with our Commonwealth Allies in Burma.

On 13 April 1944 the Chih Hui Pu and the NCAC opened their respective forward headquarters in Shaduzup. We'd come the length of the Hukawng Valley. Documents captured definitely identified elements of the 114th Regiment in front of us. That left very few troops for the defense of Myitkyina.

One April night after dinner the usual bull session started and the usual subject—women—was brought up. It was interesting to listen to the opinions of the various officers as to how this was would affect the home life of the average American, man or woman. The conclusion was that the war would wreck a lot of homes. Why? Well, what was the woman who stayed behind—with her man gone for such a long time—to do? Some of the men felt that their wives or girl friends were playing around but they couldn't prove it. Others didn't blame the women for going out because the separation was so long. Others admitted that because it was wartime they themselves would step out when and if they got the chance because the future was so uncertain. I sat and listened but didn't venture an opinion, although I thought the problem was on the mind of every man overseas.

Our headquarters at Shaduzup seemed to be a little more permanent than those at Tingkawk Sakan, Maingkwan, or Taihpa Ga. More people were joining our staff and our G-2 section was getting larger. Our quarters were improving and we finally had more than one typewriter. At Shaduzup I again met John K. Emmerson, General Stilwell's political officer. Maj. Ellis Cox, General Stilwell's son-in-law, and I occupied one of the new tents that were part of the G-2 section. Lts. Marshall Shulman and James P. Grant had joined us, and our intelligence annex was now part of the daily field order to the troops. As new officers came in to be assigned as liaison to the Chinese units, I'd been given the task of orienting them. I enjoyed this added duty and the new men seemed to be the sort General Stilwell wanted for this campaign. We also got a new signal officer. At General Stilwell's request Lt. Col. George Moynahan was transferred from Italy to take the job. As signal officer, NCAC and Chinese Army in India, he managed in a very short time to build a highly effective communications system.

It looked as though the Japanese had shot their wad at Imphal. Despite banzai charges in which whole units of up to company size were annihilated, they had been unable to take Imphal. The monsoon rains had begun, making the Japanese problem of supply and resupply almost insurmountable. Unable to bring in reinforcements, their troop strength was declining daily.

Col. Rothwell Brown's Chinese Tank Group broke through Japanese defenses north of Malakawng on 8 May, shooting up Japanese infantry and antitank positions. In addition to killing some 200 enemy and capturing seven AT guns, the group picked up some documents which we got for translation. The Chinese tankers must have hit an aid station since one of the documents dealt with such things as oxygen inhalators, collyrium, enemas, suppositories, imbrocation, and injections for the penis. From what I'd seen of the local belles, I couldn't see much use for that last item.

On 1 May big plans were being made up in General Stilwell's tent. The plans were very hush-hush and only a few of us on a need-to-know basis were privy to them. They involved Galahad, a task force composed of Merrill's Marauders and selected Chinese units organized into three combat teams. The plan, code-named End Run, was to make a dash for Myitkyina and seize the airfield there before the Japanese could react and while they were still preoccupied with Imphal and Wingate's Chindits. Combat Team K moved out on 29 April, followed a couple of days later by Combat Team H. The third combat team, known as the Mike Force, was protecting the Tetegah-tawng area for the time being. Radio silence was being maintained, and as far as I could tell, neither visitors to the headquarters nor reporters were getting any information on End Run.

It took Galahad just twenty days to reach and capture the Myit-kyina airfield. On 17 May Colonel Hunter, commanding H Force, sent the coded message, In The Ring, that let General Stilwell know Galahad had completed its mission successfully. Immediately, a company of combat engineers was sent to Mitch by glider; a battery of .50-caliber antiaircraft guns and a battalion of the 89th Chinese Regiment were sent in on C-47s. On 18 May the remainder of the 89th was flown in along with a company of 4.2 mortars and two troops of a British Bofors antiaircraft outfit. The buildup continued and by 20 May the Chinese were set to attack the town from three directions. The Marauders occupied Charpate, Pamati, and Zigzun—the road approaches to Mitch where they were supposed to remain until they could be flown back to India. Their job was done. Besides, they were a physically spent force whose effective strength was about half of what it had been when they first hit the trail out of Ledo back in February.

There was quiet jubilation back at NCAC when we got the news that Galahad had taken the airstrip at Mitch. Almost immediately, however, we began to get reports that the enemy had moved a portion of the 114th Regiment back into the town, and aerial reconnaissance showed that trenches had been dug around the perimeter on three sides. We needed a spell of good weather so we could fly in more troops and keep the Japanese from getting reinforcements by using the railroad from Mogaung. From all the intelligence we'd been able to gather, it was obvious that General Tanaka's troops were in bad shape. His two regiments had been badly mauled, first in the Hukawng Valley and now in the Mogaung Valley. We learned that elements of the 4th Regiment, 2nd Division, and the 146th Regiment, 56th Division, had been brought in piecemeal from the Salween front on the Burma-China border to assist Tanaka's 18th Division. A document turned in by the Chinese 38th Division on 18 May turned out to be an order from Maj. Gen. Toshiji Aida, Tanaka's infantry group commander, to the commander of reserves. Aida berated his junior commanders for not being more aggressive and he ordered them to destroy the enemy. At the same time he admitted that the Japanese troops were fatigued, without food, and constantly being attacked by enemy planes. He concluded by saying he would send an additional thirty men from his own headquarters staff to help if it was absolutely necessary.

Between 20 and 27 May our offensive against Myitkyina was stepped up. Elements of the Chinese 22nd and 38th divisions were preventing the enemy from reinforcing Mitch by road and trail. Additional Chinese troops had been airlifted into Mitch and we were advancing on the town from the west, south, and north.

General Stilwell committed three Chinese regiments, the 88th, 89th, and 150th, to make the assault on Myitkyina proper. Although full strength and well trained, they were not battle tested and, consequently, paid the price. They launched an attack simultaneously from the north and south of the town, but in the confusion of battle wound up shooting at each other while the Japanese withdrew to the west. The Chinese regiments also withdrew "in the face of heavy resistance," taking heavy casualties. The chance to quickly take Mitch slipped from our grasp and the battle developed into a siege that was to last until 3 August. The tired Marauders were called upon to make one last effort with only the wounded and seriously ill being flown out, while the American engineer battalions found themselves in the role of infantry. General Stilwell was able to get 3,000 replacements for his Marauders, but they were not organized or battle tested. They learned quickly! The initial elation we had felt when Col. Hunter's message came in on 17 May turned to apprehension as the days passed and it began to look as if Myitkyina might slip away from us.

On 21 May Colonel Stilwell told me he was granting me a thirty-day leave in the theater, that is, India. I had been almost eighteen months in the combat zone and was looking forward to a bit of rest. I wrote the folks at home and began to plan for 1 June.

We were getting better and better intelligence from captured documents, especially from our Chinese troops. About 1 June the Japanese battle plan for the district west of the main road came in. It detailed the actions to be taken by three battalions of the Yamazaki Butai (Task Force). The battle plan delineated the functions of squads and companies and covered the activities of the Okada Butai and the Omura Butai. It also covered passwords and day and night recognition signals and established the headquarters west of Kamaing. Needless to say, we got this to the field posthaste and the frontline units were able to take advantage of it.

We were getting more prisoners and from some incidents reported I got the impression that Japanese morale was low. Tom Ichimura told me that two of the enemy were caught when a bomb exploded near their foxhole and buried them up to their necks. They apparently decided to end it all by jabbing each other with bayonets. One of them must have had the longer arm because he stabbed his buddy although not deep enough to kill him. The stabber then tried to bite off his own tongue, but that didn't work either. They survived and we did the interrogation.

Because of the difficulties at Myitkyina, General Merrill's heart attack, Colonel McCammon's illness, and other problems, General Stilwell decided to put General Boatner in command of the Mytikyina Task Force. The force consisted of the remnants of the original Marauders, most of whom were completely burned out; the new Marauders, who fleshed out the three Marauder battalions; three Chinese regiments; two U.S. Combat Engineer Battalions, the 209th and the 236th; a British antiaircraft Bofors outfit; Seagraves' Hospital, and other assorted units for communication.

The reconstituted Marauders pushed through Namkwi, captured the north end of the north landing strip, and then entered the outskirts of Myitkyina from the north. The Chinese 42nd and 150th regiments pushed for the railroad station while the 88th and 89th regiments advanced through Charpate. Two of the Chindit LRPGs, the Morris Force and the Dah Force, had advanced from the vicinity of Hoyon and came under the operational control of the Myitkyina Task Force.

At the end of this period, about 3 June 1944, there was no more mention of my leave. As a matter of fact, my superiors seemed to be consciously avoiding the subject.

Between 3 and 10 June we progressed seven miles south and east along the axis in the Mogaung Valley, capturing eleven Japanese artillery pieces. The Chinese 22nd Division was within two miles of Kamaing and we were now assaulting the three largest towns in north Burma: Kamaing, Mogaung, and Mytikyina. The Japanese 18th Division was having trouble. They were short on rations, ammunition, and medical supplies. They were not getting any replacements and had very little air support. The Chindit 77th Brigade captured Pinhmi and Kyaingyi east of Mogaung and Ywathit to the south. They took thirty-eight prisoners in a hospital and twenty railway cars of ammunition. We got lots of stories about the prisoners from our interrogation teams. Tom Ichimura told me about one Japanese sergeant major with multiple fractures, wearing a body cast that covered half of his body, who in some way had managed to marry a local Burmese girl (or so he said) and pleaded not to be sent to a permanent POW camp in India for fear he wouldn't see her again. Tom also told me about another prisoner, a "very benevolent and cooperative chap," apparently uninjured, who took care of his sick and wounded comrades—particularly one who suffered from such severe shell shock that he was like a statue, didn't move a muscle or blink his eyes. This Japanese "Florence Nightingale" stayed awake all night keeping mosquitos away from the shell-shocked prisoner's bare body and at the same time made frequent rounds through the POW compound comforting the wounded. A morning or two later Tom walked into the stockade to do the daily head count and to his utter astonishment found the caretaker chap dead and the shell-shocked prisoner apparently recovered and lamenting over the body of his friend.

On 9 June I got sick. So ill, in fact, that I had to hit the sack. I ran a high fever, had headaches, and couldn't eat. The doctor thought I had malaria and told me to report to the hospital, but I didn't go. That same day Colonel Stilwell came to see me and told me that the Myitkyina Task Force needed an experienced intelligence officer and that I had been selected because of my experience and dual language background. There went my leave. But I felt better already and that afternoon the blood test came back negative. I packed up and got ready to leave for Mitch on the 10th.

My departure was delayed because of heavy fighting in and around Mitch and the airstrip. A Japanese prisoner was brought into Shaduzup and I went down to the stockade to talk with him. He was a twenty-nine-year-old superior private from Fukuoka with the transport regiment of the 18th Division. He was captured wandering along the road near Kwitu and surrendered willingly, unusual for a Japanese. He seemed to have above-average intelligence and talked willingly, giving us a great deal of information about the units in Mitch, their condition, strengths, and morale. He said that food, other supplies, and morale were very low, thanks to the continued bombing, strafing, and ground attacks. He estimated total troop strength in the city at between 2,000 and 2,500. If our order of battle was correct, as well as the other intelligence (part of which he corroborated) this estimate was about right.

On 12 June I finally left Shaduzup and headed for the Tingkawk Airstrip for the flight to Myitkyina. That was as far as I got because the enemy launched an attack against a Marauder battalion and came very close to retaking the airfield. I slept overnight at Tingkawk Sakan. Finally on the morning of 13 June 1944, after the usual ground fog lifted, we got the green light and took off for Mitch. I got my first look at the town as we came in for what turned out to be a touch-and-go landing. From what I could see, the Japanese lines were less than a mile from the strip and we were well within artillery range! The pilot of the little plane told me to climb out as soon as he stopped rolling and head for a bunker at the edge of the field that he quickly pointed out. (It turned out to be the Myitkyina Task Force headquarters.) The plane landed and skidded to a stop. I jumped out and the plane took off. I headed for the bunker. Myitkyina!

PART III
THE BATTLE FOR MYITKYINA

Capt. Charlie Chan with Maj. Carroll Wright, G-2 of the Myitkyina Task Force (MTF) at the Myitkyina Task Force Headquarters, Myitkyina, Burma, August 1944.

Myitkyina Task Force (MTF) Headquarters, at the airstrip, Burma, July 1944.

Captain Chan and T/5 Ralph Wilson just before a Recon flight. Myitkyina, Burma, July 1944.

USAAF Advanced Headquarters at Myitkyina Airstrip. (10th Air Force), Myitkyina, Burma, July 1944.

The airstrip at Myitkyina, Burma with the Myitkyina Task Force HQ on the right. As they looked when Myitkyina fell to General Stilwell's forces on 3 August 1944.

Bombing and artillery damage at Myitkyina.

Kim, the first "comfort girl" taken prisoner at Myitkyina. With Kim is Karl Yoneda of the OWI and a Japanese soldier. 3 August 1944.

Capt. Chan, Sgts. Howard Furumoto, Grant Hirabayashi, and Robert Honda, with Comfort Girls. Myitkyina, Burma. August 1944.

Capt. Chan and Comfort Girls with Sgt. Grant Hirabayashi. Myitkyina, Burma. August 1944.

Capt. Charlie Chan departs Myitkyina, Burma, for the United States. 22 December 1944.

Capt. Varnhagen, Maj. Jones, Capt. Chan and Bill Toy leave Myitkyina for the United States on 22 December 1944.

We Almost Had It!

H Force of Galahad, commanded by Col. Charles Hunter and consisting of the 1st Battalion of the Marauders and the 150th Regiment from the Chinese 50th Division, took possession of the Myitkyina Air Field on 17 May 1944. By 19 May the entire Galahad Task Force had encircled the town from the north, west, and south, leaving it open only toward the Irrawaddy River on the east. At this point General Merrill dissolved the Galahad Task Force and formed the Myitkyina Task Force (MTF) by reconstituting the Marauders into their original three battalions under Col. Hunter and putting the Chinese back to operating as separate regiments. The three Marauder battalions took up positions along the Namkwi River, the Mogaung-Myitkyina Railroad, and at Charpate along the road to Mogaung. The U.S. combat engineers and British AA batteries took up defensive positions at the airstrip where General Merrill established his MTF headquarters and Col. Hunter his 5307th headquarters. The Chinese 150th Regiment was to capture the town of Myitkyina, which by all estimates (later confirmed by Gen. Tanaka Shinichi, see Appendix) was held by but a few hundred Japanese troops. Attacking with two battalions, the 150th took the railroad station at the north edge of the town, but then became confused. When the Japanese withdrew, the Chinese battalions attacked each other and then withdrew to dig in defensive positions about 800 yards to the west. A battalion of the Chinese 89th Regiment had been brought into the airstrip by glider on the afternoon of the 17th, but it was not committed. The reserve battalion of the 150th, theoretically available to the commander of the regiment, had been broken up with a company at Pamati southwest of Mitch to guard approaches to the airstrip and a company securing the ferry crossing at Zigyun south of the town. The Chinese 88th Regiment had taken up defensive positions between Namkwi and Charpate. General Merrill had no forces with which to exploit the capture of the airstrip and his urgent requests to NCAC brought him another AA unit! Merrill suffered another heart attack on 22 May and was evacuated. His executive officer, Col. John McCammon, took command and made a second try with the 88th and 89th. They repeated their earlier mistakes and lost the opportunity for a quick victory in the battle for Myitkyina. The Japanese, after their initial inaction, or reaction, to the surprise attack by H Force, had time to recover and began to reinforce the Myitkyina garrison. They managed to bring troops in from as far north as Nzopzup by way of the road through Radhapur and by infiltrating through the lines of the 88th Regiment, coming from the Mogaung area. A large number came from east of the Irrawaddy and as far south as Bhamo, making their way by ferry crossings at Maingna and an undefended crossing about three miles northeast of Zigyun. By 21 May the Japanese had built up their defensive force in Myitkyina to an estimated 2,500 and were in a position to counterattack the airstrip, which they did in a series of abortive attacks through the next six to seven days.

At the Myitkyina Task Force's bunker headquarters, General Boatner saw me so I had no choice but to report directly to him. He had been in command of the MTF since 30 May when General Stilwell had relieved Colonel McCammon.

General Boatner looked very tired. His desk was strewn with maps and papers. He seemed pleased to see me, however. "Charlie," he said, "I'm giving you an additional duty. You'll be assigned to G-2, but you are to be my personal reconnaissance officer and as such I want you available to me at all times. I know that the Japanese continue to make every effort to reinforce their Myitkyina defenses by whatever means possible—road, river, railroad, infiltration. I don't have sufficient forces to block every means of access. I want you to take a liaison plane up frequently, cover all possible routes into this zone, and keep me advised." His eyes went back to the papers he'd been reading. I was clearly dismissed, so I saluted and left. In another part of the bunker I found my old friend, Maj. Alvin Larson. He was now the MTF G-1 and he filled me in on the staff structure.

I walked on past the G-3/4 bunker about seventy yards through the mud to the G-2 bunker and reported to Maj. Carroll Wright, the G-2 and my new boss. He too seemed glad to see me and told me that the enemy had mounted a company-sized attack against the 3rd Battalion of the Marauders near Charpate the night of the 11th (which was why I couldn't come in on the 12th). The 3rd Battalion, made up of a mix of original experienced Marauders and large numbers of Marauder replacements who had just arrived, beat back the attack, killing thirty in the process. The previous night a small enemy force penetrated the perimeter of the 3rd Battalion, 88th Regiment, but later withdrew. It looked like there would never be a dull moment at Mitch.

I told Maj. Wright of my meeting with General Boatner and my additional duties. He seemed a bit surprised. Apparently he had not been advised that I was to be an air observer.

I should note here that my added duties were not all that big a deal, but the way in which they were given to me pointed up once again the major problem of the CBI command channels and relationships. When the Marauders reorganized on 28 April 1944, they became part of the Galahad Task Force, a mixture of American, Chinese, and Kachin troops under the overall U.S. commander, General Merrill. Col. Charles Hunter commanded H Force, which had the 1st Battalion of the Marauders, the 150th Regiment from the Chinese 50th Division, and a battery of 75-mm pack artillery from the Chinese 22nd Division. K Force had the 3rd Battalion of the Marauders, the 88th Regiment from the Chinese 30th Division, and a battery of 75-mm pack artillery from the 5307th. M Force had the 2nd Marauder Battalion and some 300 Kachin irregulars. It was H Force that actually captured the Myitkyina Airstrip.

It was one thing to put all the Americans back together again as a provisional unit; it was another to cut loose the Chinese, two regiments from two different divisions who had been part of Galahad. Now they were essentially on their own, separate units of the MTF, but actually commanded by Chinese major generals hundreds of miles away. General Merrill's third heart attack, his forced evacuation to Ledo and replacement by Colonel McCammon didn't help. Colonel McCammon, only recently out of the hospital himself, now commanded the 5307th. He "commanded" two Chinese regiments from the 30th Division (the 88th and 89th) which were really commanded by Chinese MG Hu Shu. He "commanded" the 150th Regiment, which was actually under the command of Maj. Gen. Pan Yu-kun, commanding general of the Chinese 50th Division. He had a part of the 42nd Regiment from the 14th Division commanded by Maj. Gen. Lung Tien-wu. He also had parts of two combat engineer battalions (U.S.), a couple of AA batteries (British), and Seagraves' Hospital (U.S. and Burmese). The lines of command were not clearly drawn. Colonel McCammon had no deputy (a ranking Chinese officer would have helped) and had to deal with three Chinese division commanders in absentia in addition to one American and four Chinese regimental commanders on the scene. The failure of his Chinese units to take Myitkyina after two tries so depressed McCammon that General Stilwell was left with no choice but to relieve him. General Boatner inherited the MTF mess, but he had two advantages over McCammon.

He was a general officer, and he had commanded Chinese troops. Even so, he lasted only from 30 May to 26 June when he contracted malaria and Stilwell had to replace him with Brig. Gen. Theodore Wessels, who held the strange command until the fall of Myitkyina on 3 August.

That first night in the bunker at Mitch I couldn't sleep. The rumble of artillery fire and the crump of incoming rounds nearby kept me awake. I finally gave up, got up, and stepped outside of the bunker. As the artillery fire lit up the sky, I noticed Colonel Jacobs, the MTF G-3, standing by the entrance. For most of the night we talked and watched the Japanese fireworks, which seemed to come from gun positions south and west of the town. Jacobs and I agreed that the guns must be in the 75-mm to 77-mm range. Jacobs told me that the Japanese occasionally sent over a bomber or two. With the artillery shellings and the bombings—both aimed primarily at making the airstrip unusable—our MTF headquarter's location at the edge of the field made us sitting ducks. What's more the monsoon rains were now upon us. I could see that getting troops, rations, ammunition, and supplies could be a real problem. The C-46s and C-47s that made those runs were continually subjected to ground fire both on landing and takeoff.

Colonel Jacobs remarked that although we were inside a perimeter manned by American and Chinese troops, all of us were well inside Japanese-controlled territory. I read the G-4 report for 13 June:

> Two C-47s will drop supplies to our forces as soon as the ground fog lifts [They did]. Planes continue to draw ground fire [They do]. No serious damage reported, although one C-47 had a wing tank punctured.

By 14 June I was getting settled in. The 1st Battalion of the Marauders turned in some captured Japanese documents. From a quick translation it appeared that elements of the 148th Regiment, 56th Division (Tatsu-6737) faced the 1st Marauder Battalion positions. One 1st Battalion officer estimated the enemy strength at about 500. I did not believe this figure to be complete, although it could apply to that part of the 148th directly in front of the 1st Battalion, Marauders. On 10 June I had interrogated a prisoner at Shaduzup who estimated that between 2,000 and 2,500 Japanese troops were defending the town.

Myitkyina was a study in contradictions, as I soon found out. We knew that the Japanese were short of rations, ammunition, medical supplies, you name it. That they had a high incidence of disease and that their morale was low came to us from POWs, line-crossers, and native refugees. Yet on 16 June the 209th Engineers reported a loud-speaker to their front bellowing out in barely understandable English, "Surrender or face annihilation." Quite a switch, the Japanese using our techniques. As far as I know, no one—American or Chinese— ever surrendered to this type of broadcast.

Intelligence did pick up bits and pieces here and there. One of Detachment 101's American officers interrogated a Burmese who had made his way out of Mitch. The Burmese said that the Japanese had captured an American officer on the Sumprabum Road about thirty-five miles north of Myitkyina last February. (The Burmese notion of time is rather fuzzy, so it could have been a couple of months, give or take, either way!) The American appeared to be between twenty and twenty-five years old and from his dress "a soldier who flew in the air." The native estimated the American's weight at about eleven stone (about 155 pounds) and said the American was "tall," which to a native could be anything over 5'8". The American had a red face (all American and Europeans look that way to Asians) and light brown hair. He didn't appear to have been wounded. The native said that the American had been interrogated by Japanese intelligence at Myit-kyina—I'll bet that was an experience!—and then sent south by train.

We were getting numerous reports of enemy forces a couple of miles to our rear (to the west) at a village called Namkwi on the east bank of the Namkwi River about a mile south of the Mogaung-Myit-kyina Railroad. A Detachment 101 patrol spotted the 200- to 300-man force on 13 June. The figure was confirmed by a native line-crosser the next day.

The new Marauders, about 3,000 of them, had taken over the old 2nd and 3rd Marauder battalions. Like the original bunch, these Americans were all volunteers. Unlike their predecessors, very few had seen combat and none had trained together. They were brave and willing, but hindered by their lack of experience and unit training. Company F from the 2nd Battalion was ordered to join elements of the Chinese 42nd Regiment which had been encountering Japanese near Charpate. On the way they met a patrol of about fifty in Chinese uniforms that the young American captain commanding assumed had been sent out to guide his unit into the Chinese position. He didn't become suspicious until the Asian officer suggested that the Americans lay down their weapons and rest a bit before proceeding. Even though the American was experiencing his first (and as it turned out, his last) combat mission, he recognized an ambush when he saw one and gave the alarm. Too late. The Japanese opened up with Nambu machine guns and virtually eliminated F company. Although they fought bravely (one Pfc was awarded the DSC) very few escaped. The company was never reconstituted. The few survivors were distributed throughout the other Marauder units.

It was about this time that I met Jim Holland, who has assisted me in writing this book. Also a captain, he was the Communications Officer, 3rd Bn., 5307th, Merrill's Marauders at Myitkyina. Jim was hospitalized shortly thereafter. He returned to command a company during the Third Burma campaign, however, and later went with the 475th Infantry to Kunming, China. He returned to the States in August 1945. Jim pursued an army career, retiring as a colonel in 1967. Subsequently he took up writing as a second career.

Mine Eyes Have Seen the Glory

The sixteenth of June 1944 was a typical monsoon day in north Burma— intermittent rain with heavy overcast all the time. I decided nevertheless to pay a liaison visit to the Chinese 30th Division south and east of Namkwi near the Mogaung-Myitkyina Railroad. I checked out with the Marauder guards at the north end of the airfield perimeter and headed down the narrow jungle trail flanked by five-foot high elephant grass that made any observation except straight ahead almost impossible. I took this route because I wanted to check the condition of the defenses to our rear, then look at the area south of Namkwi and then, if possible, follow the railroad southeast toward Mitch. After taking much longer than I thought it should, I finally reached the railroad. I figured that the perimeter of the 30th should be about two miles down the tracks and it suddenly dawned on me that I was in no man's land for sure. As I moved along the jungle path that paralleled the railroad tracks, I felt alone and scared. In jungle greens with carbine in hand, I knew from past experience that I would look like a Japanese to the Chinese, the Americans, and probably the Kachins from Detachment 101. I also knew I couldn't fool the Japanese. Oh well, I thought, I wrote home yesterday.

It also crossed my mind that I was really inside Japanese-controlled territory with enemy troops all around. I remembered reading reports as late as the day before of infiltrators trying to get into Myitkyina to help the defenders and of the Detachment 101 Kachins killing Japanese south of Namkwi, which wasn't too far from where I was. Then the incident of F Company crossed my mind. The Marauders would shoot first and ask questions later. Charlie Chan, I thought to myself, you are stupid. Then as I walked along I found myself praying to God to protect me and suddenly stirring words entered my mind and I began to sing aloud, the "Battle Hymn of the Republic." I was singing a prayer asking for God's help in fighting a battle that was just. Somehow it made me feel better mentally and physically stronger, and I just knew that nothing would harm me because of my faith in God. Over and over I sang that stirring hymn until I reached the relative safety of the 30th Division perimeter and the Chinese lines. I have listened to the "Battle Hymn of the Republic" many times since that June day. Each time I hear it, my body shakes a bit and I experience an indescribable feeling. Singing that hymn or listening to it is a great personal experience. To me it combines a prayer, a feeling of patriotism, and a religious testimony all in one.

At the command post of the 30th Division I met two old friends, Lt. Cols. George Laughlin and Joe Rockis. George was now Chief Liaison Officer with the 30th Division. Joe Rockis had formerly been with the Chinese 22nd Division during the advance from Ledo. They introduced me to the senior Chinese officers at the command post. I got an excellent briefing and a look at the Japanese positions facing the 30th from the vicinity of Myitkyina. That, by the way, was only about 100 yards to our front!

I headed back to MTF headquarters at the strip before darkness set in, and needless to say, I went by a much shorter and, I hoped, safer route.

Behind the Lines: Recons and Rafts

Making observation flights was quite an experience. The Japanese in Myitkyina were only about one mile from the strip and planes of any size were subjected to ground fire both on takeoff and landing. The strip itself was made hazardous by monsoon rains and less-than-adequate maintenance because of enemy activity. This week alone two C-47s veered off the runway into water-filled ditches, both sustaining some damage to wings and undercarriage; an A-36 skidded off the end of the runway, nosed over and punctured a gas tank; and a P-40 missed the runway coming in and landed in the field to the right, damaging its wings and landing gear. Fortunately, there were no casualties in any of these incidents. The strip was still a graveyard of gliders from the mid-May airlift of Chinese troops into the area. Most of the wreckage had been bulldozed off to the side of the strip along with recently wrecked planes.

The thirty-odd observation flights I made between 14 June and 3 August were in little L-4s and L-5s, the former known as the Piper Cub. These high-winged monoplanes carried two people, had a top speed of about 125 mph, cruised at about 85 mph, could stall down to about 45 mph—making them ideal for reconnaissance missions—and could reach an altitude of about 15,000 feet allowing them to get over any hills in the area. They neither carried armament nor had any armor protection. In these planes you were a sitting duck surrounded by canvas held together with glue. Extremely light weight and with fixed landing gear, they could take off and land with a few hundred yards of runway, which sure as hell came in handy when you were being shot at!

The pilots of these little gems were usually young enlisted men of the U.S. Army Air Corps. Most were either staff or technical sergeants, although there were a few three-stripers, and an occasional junior warrant officer. Little has been written about these pilots and their activities in the CBI. Yet they flew uncounted missions over Japanese-held territory; evacuated wounded American, Chinese, British, and native troops from hastily chopped out jungle strips; and provided emergency supplies and that great morale builder, mail, which couldn't have gotten through any other way. Our light-plane support came from the 71st Liaison Squadron of the 10th Air Force. Their full complement of planes was twelve little L-4s and L-5s and the expert and dedicated mechanics usually had nine or ten operational at all times. The fifteen or so young pilots apparently flew from a roster system, so I rarely flew with the same one twice in succession. All were excellent pilots and we owed them a lot.

My job at first was to cover the routes in and out of Myitkyina for signs of enemy activity of any kind. I made two daily flights when weather permitted. On 18 June we flew south over Kazu to Nampaung along the Irrawaddy River. The only change I noted from previous flights was the absence of three native boats that had been pulled up on the river bank near Nampaung. Probably fishing boats, but I reported it anyway, you never know. On the morning of the 19th we followed the railroad line from the yards in Mitch as far west as Namkwi where we observed work in progress to repair the railroad bridge over the Namkwi Hka. We also drew ground fire from three Japanese who were in a foxhole nearby. When we got back to the strip we found a couple of bullet holes in the fuselage of our little Cub, but neither the pilot nor I was hit. Our afternoon flight that same day took us along the same railroad, but this time all the way to Mogaung. I found the tracks to be serviceable though there was no traffic and a small bridge over a tributary of the Namkwi Hka was still down. We saw no signs of enemy activity. On the 20th we again followed the railroad to Mogaung, backtracked to Namkwi, picked up the Myitkyina-Sumprabum Road, and followed it as far as Nzopzup. Then we again doubled back, going south of Mitch to the Kazu-Talawgyi area. No movement. No nothing. Our flights on 21 June covered the Namkwi area again. Work on the bridge had apparently ceased as had work on the road that linked Charpate, Mankrin, and Saungka. Again, nothing to report and I began to wonder if all this was worth the effort. However, that afternoon when we headed east and south of Mitch, I saw a loaded truck heading toward Washaung, two empty trucks moving toward Waingmaw, twenty native boats, and four rafts floating downstream on the Irrawaddy near Khaungpu and evidence of troop movement in the area. On the 21st while doing a repeat run, we again saw a truck on the road from Waingmaw to Washaung. We took our Cub down low as the truck ran off the road and under a tree. Three men in blue uniforms (marines?) jumped in a ditch and took shelter. Although we were less than 600 feet above them, they made no attempt to fire at us.

What happened to all the information we obtained and reported? To this day I don't really know. I do know that our recon and observation flights pretty well confirmed that no Japanese reinforcements (at least not in any large numbers) were getting into Myitkyina. Neither were supplies and ammo for that matter, nor did many people seem to be leaving except a few refugees and line-crossers, and occasionally sick and wounded on rafts. General Boatner must have taken some encouragement from this. To be available to the general I had a small dugout in the rear of the MTF headquarters bunker which contained a canvas cot and an empty, turned-up ammunition box—my home away from home for the duration.

With only Major Wright, Lieutenant Tenney, and me in the G-2 section of the Myitkyina Task Force, we all worked virtually around the clock. Wright attended the staff meetings where he gave the G-2 portion of the daily briefing sessions. He was also called on to give separate briefings to whatever visiting firemen were audacious enough to drop in at MTF and there were a few. He did the necessary coordinating with the G-3 and the A-2/3 attached to MTF from the USAAF. Ed Tenney minded the store, keeping in daily contact with and receiving reports from the Peers Group (Det. 101), the British Morris Force, the Marauder units, the U.S. Combat Engineers, the Kachin Levies, and the American liaison officers from the Chinese divisions and regiments. My first priority, of course, was to fly General Boatner's recon missions. I also did the initial prisoner interrogations and translated captured documents. Never a dull moment as we tried to keep everyone from General Stilwell and General Boatner on down abreast of the enemy situation. Oh yes, don't forget that daily G-2 roundup to which all three of us contributed.

By 23 June 1944 it began to look like the enemy was concentrating on getting the sick and wounded out of Myitkyina by way of the Irrawaddy River. A Marauder patrol reported killing two Japanese on an oil-drum raft. The Japanese went overboard into the river, but the patrol found six rifles and a sack of rice on the raft. Chinese of the 50th Division reported firing on four rafts in the same area while another Marauder patrol near Pamati reported killing three Japanese, also on an oil-drum raft. Reports from the liaison officers with the 50th Division spoke of rafts, some with huts constructed on them, floating down the river south of Myitkyina. No report of anyone on board any of them. Further south and west near Pamati troops of the 150th Regiment claim to have killed twelve Japanese on rafts. More unoccupied rafts were also observed. On the 23rd during one of my recon flights I picked up eight to ten native boats at Khaungpu as well as three more boats and a large raft near Talawgyi. Were the rats trying to desert a sinking ship? It looked like it.

Among prisoners taken by the Chinese 88th Regiment were two Chinese who claimed to have been impressed into service by the Japanese at Myitkyina. They were armed and serving the outer defense line. I was surprised that they hadn't been summarily executed by the

Chinese Pings. Under questioning they said that some supplies for the Mitch garrison were coming from a dump some forty miles to the east of Mitch, being ferried across the Irrawaddy near Waingmaw. They claimed that the Myitkyina defense force consisted of about 600 Japanese and about 400 Burmese and Chinese. Myitkyina was ringed by four defense lines, no withdrawal was planned, and no reinforcements were expected. If true, this was a grim report from the Japanese standpoint.

Through 24 June we continued to get reports from natives, U.S. units, Chinese units, and Ray Peers' 101 people concerning Japanese activity in the vicinity of Mitch. Many of the reports were conflicting and difficult to corroborate, but we tried. Some natives reported boats and rafts apparently being readied to evacuate Mitch, while other reports stated that about 500 Japanese got into Mitch on foot by way of the road from Charpate, while another fifty came in from Saungka. Who to believe and how far to believe them?—G-2's life is not a happy one.

We Advance Slowly

A G-3 situation report makes for prosaic reading and doesn't tell very much to anyone but the man who wields the black and red grease pencils on acetate-covered maps. But those same maps are crucial to senior officers at NCAC in Shaduzup, at U.S. Army CBI headquarters in New Delhi, and at SEAC in Kandy, Ceylon, to determine the big picture. From 25 June to 1 July 1944, the NCAC report stated that the 2nd Battalion, 5307 had replaced the 3rd Battalion, 5307 astride the Sumprabum Road north of Sitapur; 3rd Battalion, 5307 replaced the 2nd Battalion, 5307 for defense of the Myitkyina Airstrip and MTF headquarters. (So far no problems, just change the symbols on the map.) 2nd Battalion, 5307 attacked south toward Sitapur, making limited gains; the 209th Engr (C) Battalion advanced 100 yards on the right flank of the 2nd Battalion, 5307; 236th Engr (C) Battalion advanced 100 yards south along the Myitkyina-Mogaung Road. (Limited? 100 yards? Hell, that wouldn't even show on the scale maps being used at the higher headquarters. Just leave 'em where they are.) The report went on to say that air support was very limited due to adverse weather conditions.

What the report didn't say and what the maps couldn't show was just how precarious our situation at Myitkyina really was. The physical condition of the old Marauders was deteriorating more and more day by day. The new Marauders were becoming acclimated and learning their jobs, but the lessons were slow and painful. The two battalions of combat engineers were not battle-tested combat infantry; and the Chinese, the numerically largest force we had, were still in the process of shaking down, being "blooded" as the saying goes, and learning their jobs. All of these forces were up against the battle-wise, tough Japanese veterans of Malaya and Singapore.

"Air support was very limited" said the report—and we were totally dependent on air support for our very survival. Rations, ammunition, medical and other supplies, weapons replacements, and human replacements all had to get to us by air. After initial treatment by either Seagraves' Field Hospital Unit with those brave Burmese nurses or by the 42nd Portable Field Hospital, all seriously wounded or sick people had to be evacuated by air to hospitals in India. During the days of late May and throughout June, we literally hung on by the skin of our teeth. Had the Imperial Japanese Air Force been able to mount an all-out effort against us at Mitch, the final outcome undoubtedly would have been different. They did try, but just didn't have the strength after Imphal and the Arakan. Still, we took some flak. On 29 June at 0645 hours three Zeros attacked one of our C-47 supply planes that was en route to China and flying past Myitkyina at about 14,000 feet. Three of the U.S. airmen aboard bailed out and were later picked up by Kachins of the Morris Force east of the Irrawaddy. The C-47 crashed in flames, possibly with the pilot still aboard. The following day, 30 June, six Zeros attacked an inbound C-47 about ten minutes from the field. One airman was seriously wounded while the plane lost a part of its left wing, its radio was knocked out and a tire punctured. Nevertheless, the pilot brought the plane in safely except for a couple of bent propellers. Our P-40 fighters responded quickly and the Japanese didn't stay around very long. This spate of air activity didn't do much for the morale of those of us who flew the liaison-recon missions. With each succeeding flight, we strained our eyes skyward and groundward with increased intensity, on a "fifty-fifty" basis, that is, I looked for activity on the ground while the pilot looked for it in the air and then vice versa.

Gen. Theodore F. Wessels who had relieved Gen. Boatner on 26 June was quite concerned about the possibility of enemy reinforcements for Mitch coming from the vicinity of Bhamo, so we flew a number of sorties along the trace of the Myitkyina-Bhamo Road. Unfortunately, tall trees growing along the sides of the road formed an overhead canopy that made observation of the road itself virtually impossible, even at extremely low altitudes, except when a trail or stream intersected the road. Even in these instances the monsoon rains had left the trails so muddy that determining if there had been recent movement was largely guesswork. The streams, like the rivers into which they flowed, were swollen, spilling over their banks to a point where if there had been anything of intelligence value to observe it had long since disappeared.

One flight, however, did give me a real thrill. On 28 June 1944 at about 1100 hours we swung east of the Myitkyina-Bhamo Road on our way back to the Mitch strip. The pilot alerted me over the intercom and pointing down and toward the east he said, "Captain Chan, that's China." Almost twenty-nine years after my entry into this world in the United States of America, I had my first glimpse of the land of my ancestors—China! It didn't look much different—at least not at 4,000 feet—than the terrain of Burma, but it was China and I was thrilled with the sight. Back at MTF headquarters, I used a map to pinpoint the Chinese village of Lienshan that I had been looking down on.

Our recon flights continued to cover all the approaches to Mitch but with negative results. Oh, there was occasionally a single truck to be seen, usually alongside the road and apparently empty. No troop movements, however, and there was no evidence of repair activity at the bridges over the Namkwi Hka or its tributaries. On 28 June we received six wounded prisoners from Mogaung. The town had fallen on 27 June. The POWs were all privates, in poor physical condition, and of little or no intelligence value.

The 5307th picked up two more, one on 29 June, who was wounded, and one who voluntarily surrendered on 30 June. The first one, who died shortly after capture, was from the 2nd Company, 1st Battalion, 114th Regiment, which he said had been sent from Mitch in January 1944 to patrol north along the Sumprabum Road. When captured, he and what was left of his company were carrying artillery shells from a small dump north of Sitapur into Myitkyina. As far as he knew, there were no Japanese forces left along the Myitkyina-Sumprabum Road. The one who surrendered confirmed this information. He said he had beriberi and had been hospitalized near the ten-mile mark on the Myitkyina-Sumprabum Road. When the enemy defenses collapsed under repeated attacks from the 5307th, hospital patients were told to escape as best they could. He had been a rifleman in the 2nd Plt, 3rd Co., 55th Reg't in Mitch and was headed back that way. He said morale had been very low among the Myitkyina garrison when he had been sent to the hospital about two weeks earlier.

We asked the 5307th and the Chinese 50th Division to estimate the number of enemies they had killed at Mitch since the operation began in May. The Americans estimated a nice round figure of 500. The Chinese were more precise, estimating that they had killed 436 while wounding 873!

As of 1 July we were getting almost daily reports from Det. 101 patrols, Morris Force patrols, and native informants regarding the movements of small enemy forces along the road from Washaung; and on 1 July the 5307th caught about thirty Japanese, less than a half-mile northeast of their headquarters. After the action, they counted twenty-eight Japanese dead with a number of those apparently being suicides. One prisoner was taken and a number of Indian coolies surrendered. They had apparently been trying to get some 75-mm ammo from a dump near the airstrip into Mitch.

The 2 to 8 July 1944 NCAC situation report read in part: 150th Reg't captured several Japanese strongpoints [thus] strengthening their forward line in the sector; 42nd and 89th Reg'ts made limited gains; 88th Reg't repelled heavy night attacks; 236th Eng'r (C) Bn with the 209th Eng'r (C) Bn (-) attached maintained its roadblock astride the Myitkyina-Sumprabum Road near Radhapur; Co C, 209th Eng'r (C) Bn was attached to 2nd Bn, 5307th patrolling north and northwest of Myitkyina. B-25s from the 10th USAAF continued to pound the town.

A rather bland report that didn't say much and certainly didn't cause the grease-pencil boys any problems. Nevertheless, action in and around Mitch continued hot and heavy. While the Pings and GIs were making progress by the yard, slugging it out on the ground, the Japanese made their presence felt increasingly in the air. Planes with the red meatball on their tails were around us every day. Three showed up on 2 July, three more on 3 July, but made no attempt to strafe or bomb. On 5 July, however, twelve Zeros broke through the clouds over Waingmaw undetected because they were flying at an extremely low altitude. They strafed the positions of the Chinese 42nd and 150th regiments south of the town then flew over the town and the northern areas, dropping four or five colored parachutes probably of medical or other supplies as they sped away. None of our fighters had been in the air at the time and the AA batteries couldn't react in time. On 6 July three planes again approached the airstrip, but this time we had been alerted and our fighters drove them off. On 7 July eight Zeros flew in—again undetected—at about 800 feet altitude, from the direction of Waingmaw. The leader was a Tojo, the others were Zekes, Oscars, and Hamps. They made their run from south to north, dropping about 150 antipersonnel and antimaterial bombs that weighed about one-and-a-half pounds each. Fortunately for us, ninety percent of the bombs were duds and did not explode. We found out later that the wind-driven tail mechanisms were corroded, probably because of outside storage. Again, none of our fighters had been in the air and seven of them on the ground received some damage from 20-mm cannon and .51-caliber machine guns when the zeros made a couple of passes over the strip. After the second pass they wheeled and headed south toward Waingmaw. The British AA gunners claimed hitting at least one of the Zeros, but as far as we could tell all the planes got away.

On 5 July 1944 it happened. (As I had known it would ever since I started making these observation runs in mid-June.) We were coming back from a check of the Myitkyina-Bhamo Road. The pilot told me that a red alert had been sounded at the strip. We kept our eyes peeled for enemy aircraft but saw none. After flying past Mitch we circled back to the left and started our descent to the field. At about 200 feet up and maybe 500 yards from the end of the strip, all hell started to break loose as ack-ack shells began to burst all around us. The twelve Japanese planes that had strafed the Chinese were now dropping parachutes over the town and our British AA gunners were doing their best to shoot them down—with our little L-4 caught in the crossfire! The pilot poured on the coal, putting the Cub in a steep climb and a sharp bank to the right in order to get away from the action. We remained airborne spectators at a safe distance until the

Japanese completed their airdrop and cleared out of the area. When MTF finally sounded the all clear we came in for a safe landing, almost on a wing and a prayer and out of fuel.

The radio operator of the C-47 shot down on 29 June was rescued by a Kachin patrol from the Morris Force and brought to MTF headquarters on 2 July. He had parachuted safely, landing near the Irrawaddy River north of Myitkyina. A couple of hundred yards from where he landed he stumbled onto a deserted basha, well stocked with Japanese canned rations that he lived on for three days before the Kachins found him. The pilot of this same C-47 had not gone down with his plane but had parachuted safely only to be picked up by Burmans who turned him over to a Japanese patrol (for cash?). It was reported that the pilot was then taken to Myitkyina and summarily executed. Two days later the Morris Kachins picked up the three Burmese who had turned the American pilot over to the Japanese. The Kachins killed the three Burmese on the spot—an eye for an eye. This was a vicious war. Wreckage of the C-47 was spotted by one of our L-5 pilots and a Morris patrol was able to salvage some of the cargo and the instruments.

I continued my recon flights along all possible access (or withdrawal) routes to Mitch but with negative results. Maybe the Japanese were just going to fight it out from their defensive positions around the city. They had two 75-mm field guns at Mitch that they use sparingly (probably because of a shortage of ammo) but judiciously. They knew our eating habits and invariably dropped a few rounds on us with almost Dr.-Pepper precision: 7, 12, and 5! On 6 July, for example, they fired thirteen rounds beginning at noon, killing one Chinese and wounding two others. Despite the best efforts of our spotters, fighters, and bombers, we were not able to silence these guns until the very end of the campaign and then only by ground action. The Chinese troops overran one gun on 25 July. The remaining gun kept up sporadic firing until captured by the 3rd Battalion of the 5307th on 3 August, the day the town was officially declared ours.

Although our recon flights weren't turning up much during this period, we were getting a plethora of reports from the Morris Force, 101 Force, 5307 patrols, Chinese patrols, line-crossers and refugees coming out of Myitkyina, and an occasional POW. Nothing beat on-the-ground observation, although sometimes a follow-up aerial recon to a patrol or native report was helpful. On 7 July, a Peers patrol reported finding a series of Japanese listening posts paralleling the Myitkyina-Sumprabum Road. We again made a recon flight of the area and this time spotted a clearing in the dense jungle from which patrol routes were clearly discernable.

From the interrogation of POWs and the questioning of line-crossers and refugees, it would appear that some of the soldiers of the 114th Regiment who were sent north out of Myitkyina in May were still trying to get back in. We had also received a report about a possible new weapon in the area, a 75- or 76-mm mortar, breech loading, firing an artillery-type shell from a base plate but without sights. This, I wanted to see. We had asked both the Chinese and American troops to be on the lookout for this strange baby. (But we never did locate such a weapon.) While our talks with prisoners and others indicated that some were trying to get back into Mitch, reports from our forces told of rafts on the Irrawaddy heading away from Mitch along with much cutting of bamboo by the Japanese to build more rafts. (Sounds like President Roosevelt's WPA—two comin', two goin', two stayin'.)

The 9 to 15 July 1944 NCAC situation report on the Myitkyina Task Force read like a repetition of previous reports:

> 150th Reg't pushed forward strongly; 42nd Reg't captured part of the Myitkyina Railroad yards; all [Chinese] units advanced against stubborn resistance; elements of the 5307th and the 209-236 Engineer Combat Battalions straightened their lines; B-25s continued to bomb Myitkyina, Waingmaw, and Maingna.

We were engaged in siege warfare—rough, tough, and dirty. The Japanese might be low on morale, but they were well dug in, tenacious fighters. They were forcing the Pings and the GIs to battle to the utmost for every inch of ground. I'd watched some of our Chinese and American combat patrols returning: dirty, mud-caked, tired to the point of exhaustion, their gaunt bodies and hollow-eyed faces reflecting the physical and mental suffering they must have been going through.

Japanese air activity continued to be heavy. On 9 July at noon some fifteen to eighteen fighters attacked the strip. As usual they came in from the south at a low altitude and began to circle the field coun-terclockwise, strafing and dropping antipersonnel bombs. They were the usual mixture of Zero types: Tojos, Oscars, Zekes, and Hamps. This time, however, they were detected about five minutes out from the strip and a flight of four of our P-40s got in the air to intercept and engage them. It was a real thrill to watch this aerial battle. Three of the Zeros crashed in flames, victims of the P-40s and the British ack-ack gunners. I counted seven other Zeros fleeing the scene with black smoke streaming from them. It was difficult to tell where they all went, but we heard later that a flight of P-51s from Shaduzup caught up with some of them about thirty miles south of us and knocked out at least one and probably two more. Three of the P-40s suffered minor damage but managed to land safely. Box score: U.S. 6—En-emy 0! While the air battle was in progress, those pesky 75s sent about ten rounds into the west side of the strip very close to our head-quarters. No casualties and negligible damage to us on the ground from either the planes or the artillery, but the banshee whine of the Zeros as they dived, the staccato rattle of the 20-mm cannon and machine guns, and the crump of artillery shells as they landed wasn't conducive to a pleasant lunch.

We had alerts again on the 10th and 11th, but no Japanese planes showed up. The 5307th reported that natives were seen east of the Irrawaddy at Pamati waving turbans and head cloths when the planes appeared on the 9th. I doubt if this was more than the Burmese en-couraging the Japanese. The pilots sure as hell knew where Mitch was by then! I continued my observation flights at the direction of General Wessels (who succeeded Boatner), but with special attention to the water approaches to Myitkyina, the Irrawaddy in particular. Several of us spotted unoccupied rafts along the banks of the river during the next few days. The rafts were new, fairly large (maybe fifteen by eight feet), well made of bamboo, and fitted with raised oarlocks at the bow and stern for sculling. Natives reported to us that the Japanese intended to use them to evacuate their sick and wounded from Myitkyina to Kathyo very soon. Maybe the end of this long hard battle for Myitkyina was in sight. Of course we also continued to cover road, trail, and railroad approaches to Mitch as well, but only an occasional single vehicle was spotted, no troop movements or concentrations. Both the Americans and the Chinese were taking an increasing number of prisoners. We got fourteen beetween 11 and 14 July. Many were seriously ill with malaria, mite typhus, and beriberi. Two died of their wounds before they could be interrogated. Surprisingly, most were attempting to get into not out of Myitkyina.

    After repeated requests from Maj. Wright, we finally got some help. Colonel Stilwell sent Tom Ichimura and Yas Koike to the Myitkyina Task Force G-2 to give us a hand. Their initial baptism of fire is worth noting. Tom Ichimura put it this way:

We came down from Shaduzup in one of General Stilwell's C-46s that seemed pretty plush to a couple of GIs used to those metal bucket seats, no heat, and no insulation. As we were making our final approach, we could see that the field was pockmarked with potholes, apparently from incoming artillery, and was a veritable graveyard of downed planes and gliders. As we jumped out of the plane that brought us in, another landed, hit a pothole and ground looped. A few of us ran toward it hoping to get anyone out that might have been trapped inside. We could see the pilot slumped in the cockpit. There was a strong smell of AvGas and an explosion was a distinct possibility. Some GI who had gotten there before us was trying (by using a hacksaw) to cut off a metal rod imbedded in the pilot's leg. He cut through the rod and we were able to lift the unconscious flyer out of the plane. We made sort of a carrier from a used parachute and got the injured pilot to a bunker on the west side of the field as artillery shells began to land all around us.

    We left the pilot to the medics while Yas and I took off with a GI guide to another bunker where a group of enemy soldiers was supposed to be holed up. Our mission: talk 'em into surrendering. By the time we got there, however, the Chinese Pings had solved the problem—all were dead. Now we had to get ourselves back to MTF headquarters without our being killed by those same Pings before we could be identified as American GIs. The GIs of the 5307th solved this problem. They formed sort of a British square with Yas and me in the middle and moving almost in lock-step we made it.

Nothing like diving into battle head first! Like all the Nisei who served their country in the front lines, Tom and Yas served well.

Ichimura and Koike arrived at the MTF G-2 at a most critical time. Their interrogation, translation, and linguistic skills were certainly needed and they immediately plunged in, working eighteen to twenty hour days like the rest of us, under enemy fire and certainly not under the best of conditions! We were too close to the Myitkyina perimeter to hold captured Japanese soldiers very long. When prisoners were placed in the makeshift MP holding area at the airstrip, Tom and Yas would immediately scurry over and conduct spot interrogations almost before the shelling stopped so that the POWs could be evacuated to the rear. Following the fall of Myitkyina, Tom and Yas were reassigned to Theater G-2 in Delhi, but both returned to Burma in February 1945 to take part in the conclusion and aftermath of the Third Burma campaign.

More POWs, as well as line-crossers—Indians and Shan-Burmans—escaping from Mitch told of near famine in the town. It couldn't last too much longer.

Colonel Jacobs was replaced by my friend Col. George T. Laughlin as the G-3 of MTF. With his experience as the senior liaison officer with the Chinese 30th Division, he would do well.

We were not encircled anymore. The fall of Mogaung and the clearing of the enemy from the Mogaung-Myitkyina Railroad took care of our rear and we could concentrate our total effort towards the front: Myitkyina.

Myitkyina Falls

Refugees were fleeing Mitch in increasing numbers. They could get out now, they told us, because many segments of the outer perimeter were loosely manned and the perimeter had many gaps. These natives also talked of low morale among General Mizukami's veteran troops, even an occasional suicide. Medical supplies were almost non-existent, food was rapidly running out, and so was ammunition. The ill and wounded who could walk and hold a rifle were being put in the defensive lines, and there was also an intensive raft-building program.

Rafts seemed to be the big thing with the Japanese those days. Some thirty-nine natives who managed to get out of Sitapur said that they had been used as forced labor to cut bamboo and construct rafts.

Natives also confirmed other reports of low morale, food, and ammo in and around Mitch.

About sixty-four Japanese tried to get from Saungka to Myitkyina by raft but were attacked by the 2nd Bn, 5307th on 19 July.

A lieutenant and thirty-three enlisted men were taken prisoner, twenty-eight were reported killed. I interrogated the lieutenant. He said that all on the raft had been patients at a military hospital near Saungka. They were ordered to get to Myitkyina or to Namti on the Myitkyina-Mogaung Railroad line. He didn't know that Mogaung had fallen. Another hundred able-bodied patients (unarmed) and fifty hospital guards and medics (some armed) were walking out of Saungka toward Mitch, while another group of 100 (he thought it was a company) were supposed to be headed for Mitch from Nzopzup.

Four more rafts, all apparently empty, were reported by the Chinese 50th Division on 21 July. Another well-constructed but empty raft was located by a river patrol from the 1st Bn, 5307th at Zigyun on an island in the river directly south of Mitch. It had a machine-gun mount but no weapon as well as built-in compartments for storing equipment. Native line-crossers stated that the Japanese had impressed native labor to build a raft every three days at a village about a mile east of the Irrawaddy on the Namyin Hka. In addition they had ordered 1,000 Pungyi sticks: bamboo sticks about one-and-a-half-feet long that are sharpened to a point, impregnated with poison, and used in booby traps.

A lone sergeant was captured 22 July rafting from Mitch toward Waingmaw. He told me he had last seen Col. Maruyama in Myitkyina about 9 July and that the colonel appeared in good health. The sergeant also estimated the effective strength of the Mitch garrison at about 500 with maybe another 200 sick and wounded. The garrison, he said, was a mixed bag of troops from the 114th Regiment, mountain artillery from the 18th Division (I wondered if they handled those 75-mms that were so damned pesky?), elements from the 56th Division and a number of miscellaneous units he couldn't or wouldn't identify. He wouldn't say where he'd been or what he'd been doing between 9 and 22 July.

I stepped up my aerial observation of the Irrawaddy, often going up when I got a gut feeling that I'd find some activity. We spotted a lot of what appeared to be floating trees and logs, the latter looking like those I'd seen during logging operations on the rivers back home in Oregon. However, when these "trees and logs" headed for the banks of the river to get under the overhanging jungle growth as our little plane approached, I realized we'd been looking at some very carefully and cleverly camouflaged rafts. It was virtually impossible to spot people when they're hidden this way. From then on I notified the Morris and Peers Forces of my observations. If there were any enemy military on those rafts, I'm sure they got a warm reception farther south along the river.

By 21 July 1944 there was no question in my mind that the tide of battle was running in our favor. The Japanese were on the ropes, going down for the count, but they were not out yet. Of the two 75-mm field pieces that had been pestering us for over two months, one still remained. It stayed zeroed in on MTF headquarters firing from different locations within the perimeter. The GIs and Pings were getting careless about dispersing when they lined up for chow and at noon the enemy gun crew sent ten rounds over in rapid succession, scattering soldiers in all directions. As the first two or three shells impacted, I dropped my mess kit and, bent over running like the wind, I zigzagged my way to where the light planes were revetted. Grabbing a pilot we got airborne and tried to locate the firing position before the shells stopped coming in. We didn't do it that day nor did we do it on numerous tries after. By the time we were in the air the gun crew had fired their allotment for the day and concealed the gun.

One time I tried getting airborne just before chow time, hoping to catch the crew moving the gun out. No such luck. They probably saw me first and didn't come out. At least the GIs and Pings got to eat in peace that particular day. We played this cat and mouse game right to the very end. That pesky gun continued to fire until it was overrun by GIs from the 3rd Bn, 5307th on the north airstrip not far from Sitapur on 3 August. It had been manhandled all over the perimeter for seventy-eight days and must have fired 500 rounds. While it hadn't inflicted heavy damages, it had affected our morale and certainly had frustrated our efforts to find it. I made it a point to go look at that gun after the battle was over just so I could say I'd seen it.

With the rapidly deteriorating situation within the perimeter, we were trying psychological warfare again. The Office of War Information (OWI) was supervising, but the effort was being carried out by a tall, skinny American from Colorado and a tall, thin Nisei from

Seattle, Washington. Every evening John K. Emmerson, a career for-eign-service officer and one of the political advisors to General Stil-well, teamed up with Japanese American Sgt. Henry Gosho to try to talk the besieged Myitkyina garrison into surrendering. According to Nisei, as well as POWs I talked with, Emmerson's Japanese was nearly perfect. POWs I talked with said they couldn't believe that the voices they heard were those of an American from the plains of the American West and a Japanese American from Seattle!

Special orders #196, paragraph 13, finally made it official on 14 July 1944:

> The VOCG, dtd 1 Jul 44 pursuant to auth contained in ED AGO ltr 21C.49 (24 Jul 43) OB-S-SPFM1-M dtd 5 Aug 43, Capt Won-loy Chan, 0-342689, FA, NCAC, is required to participate reg-ularly and frequently in aerial flights for the period 1 Jul 44 to 31 Jul 44, both dates inclusive, is confirmed and made a matter of record.

Nothing said about those flights between 13 and 30 Jun 44 directed by General Boatner but at least I'm on the record!

I continued my reconnaissance flights, right up to 3 August 1944 and the fall of Myitkyina to our forces. I covered the same terrain over and over again: the Bhamo run by road and river from Mitch south to Bhamo and back again, the Sumprabum Road north from Sitapur over Radhapur and Mankrin with an occasional diversion to Charpate and Namkwi, special attention to the Irrawaddy from north of Maingna past Mitch to Waigmaw, then following the tortuous bends of the river west past Zigyun, Katkyo, and Pamati before turning south again toward Bhamo. It got to be monotonous with all the flights producing negative results: no troop or vehicle movements, no troop concentrations. The Japanese were leaving Mitch, we were certain of that, probably under cover of darkness, and as far as we could tell no replacements were getting in.

By 23 to 29 July 1944 it was strictly street fighting in Myitkyina. The Japanese were being squeezed against the river as the Chinese pushed from south to north and from west to east. The Americans were applying pressure from north to south and also west to east.

Other American forces sat astride the Sumprabum, Mogaung, and Bhamo roads as well as the Myitkyina-Mogaung Railroad, effectively closing any escape routes or access routes. Our B-25s were still pounding the center of the town.

On 23 July General Wessels received a native report of enemy soldiers seen to the rear of the 5307th perimeter northeast of the rice paddy area. I immediately got myself airborne and checked out the area thoroughly, cajoling the pilot to skim in well below the pre-scribed safety altitude. We saw movement and the flashes of rifle fire. Landing after a few minutes in the air, we found that our little L-5 had more holes in its wings and fuselage than a Swiss cheese—for-tunately, the pilot and I didn't. We passed the word to the 5307th and that night one of their patrols flushed out the enemy, killing nine of them. How many there were, the natives said twenty-five, we would never know for sure. Whether they were trying to get in or out of Mitch or were a combat patrol setting up an ambush, we would never know either, although my best guess was that they were trying to get out. With the critical shortages of food, medicines, supplies, and ammo in Mitch, I couldn't imagine anyone wanting to get in. With the large number of rafts both observed and reported being built, the poorly manned perimeter, the many prisoners being taken (some wounded and some voluntarily surrendering), and the steady stream of refugees coming out of the town unchecked, it began to look more and more like the end was really near. Three Japanese soldiers picked up by a Shan-Burman village headman were suffering from wounds. They told me that wounded men were being placed on rafts, given three days' rations, and told to get to Bhamo if they could. We were getting more reports of suicides, mostly by grenades, and at least one Japanese had surrendered because of the psywar broadcasts. He said he liked the Japanese songs. I didn't know that John Emmerson or Hank Gosho could sing!

All reports coming in between 25 and 29 July 1944 read alike regardless of the source. Rafts were going downriver day and night; persons aboard the rafts were being either killed or captured; fourteen rafts and three motorboats sighted, 116 killed, thirty-four prisoners taken, 131 refugees coming into our lines in less than a week. A number of the prisoners were badly wounded, some still wearing filthy, bloody bandages and some with equally filthy plaster casts on their legs or arms. This further confirmed reports we'd had from refugees and line-crossers that the Japanese were being forced to return mobile wounded and sick to frontline duty. From the miasma that drifted from the vicinity of Mitch when the wind was right, it was also apparent that they were leaving their dead unburied. Nevertheless, with General Mizukami and Colonel Maruyama still directing the defensive effort, the fighting went on. The defenders were reported to be moving from one position to another to give the impression of a greater strength than they actually had and to be using bamboo to simulate automatic weapons firing. The beating of dry bamboo does sound like the firing of the Nambu machine gun.

I continued my recon flights, but as of 27 July I'd found no activity anywhere either toward or from Myitkyina.

On 25 July I wrote home:

It's been raining all night and this dugout I call home is full of dirty, muddy water this morning. I'll have to bail it out somehow or not sleep. The Japanese continue to shell us, but it doesn't bother me as much as it used to. It will soon be 20 months since I steamed out of San Francisco on the *Île de France*. I do get depressed and disgusted now and then and sometimes I think I'll go nuts, not from the shelling, but from living in filth, dirt, mud, and the constant rain plus being exposed to malaria, mite typhus, jungle rot, and snakes—I hate snakes.

It was all but over. We were measuring our advances in hundreds and thousands of yards now. On 30 July the Chinese 150th Regiment completely overran Japanese defenses in the southeast part of Mitch advancing 2,000 yards north along the Irrawaddy to just south of Sitapur. The 3rd Bn, 5307th moved east from the south end of the north airstrip, joined the 2nd Bn and together they advanced 3,000 yards south, clearing the Sitapur area. The town of Myitkyina was officially declared to be in Allied hands on 3 August 1944 when all organized resistance ceased. Small pockets of holdouts were mopped up and all resistance ceased by 5 August.

I was fortunate to be able to listen in on the planning for the final assault. General Wessels, Colonel Willey (the chief of staff), Colonel Laughlin (the G-3), and others discussed methods with Gen. Pan Yukun, commander of the Chinese 50th Division. They decided that a number of Chinese raiding parties would infiltrate Myitkyina the night of 2 August to take up positions in the rear of the Japanese defensive lines to create confusion and havoc when the final assault took place on 3 August. The final attack began at 0430 hours on the morning of 3 August led by elements of the Chinese 50th Division. The Chinese 14th and 30th divisions conducted holding actions on the west and south of the doomed town while the Americans of the 5307th did the same in the north. By 1545 hours, some thirteen hours later, Myitkyina was ours.

A few hours before the end, Maj. Carroll Wright and I grabbed a jeep and with carbines at the ready took off for the town we'd been looking at for the past fifty-five days. We advised the chief of staff we were going and told him we would advise all units that a POW collection point would be in operation at the airfield. Considering that Colonel Stilwell had recalled Ichimura and Koike to NCAC forward headquarters at Shaduzup on 1 August that was a pretty rash statement. We also promised an Administrative Order #1 on the handling of POWs, documents, and refugees. Shorthanded and with POWs, documents, and refugees descending on us from virtually everywhere in the Myitkyina area, I don't remember ever seeing such an administrative order, but we got the job done. Major Wright and I picked up the Pamati-Myitkyina Road southeast of the airstrip and after driving northeast about a quarter of a mile, we entered the outskirts of the town. The ruins were still smoldering and the stench of unburied bodies left too long in the subtropical sun was overpowering. Our flyboys had really done a job. The 500 pounders of the B-25s had left few buildings intact and through the ruins we could see the underground tunnels and bunkers that had been part of the final defensive positions. Even the basements of temples had been used. We drove through the deserted streets past burned-out vehicles, discarded weapons, and unburied dead for about an hour. Because of the danger of booby traps, we confined our observations to what we could see from the jeep. We retraced our route back to MTF headquarters where Major Wright reported to Wessels while I immediately began the processing of POWs, who were being brought in in increasing numbers. Documents were being turned in also, but I had to assign them a lower priority. Of the prisoners brought in on 3 August, none attracted more attention and curiosity than did a young Korean female who answered to the name of Kim. Morris Force Kachins had captured her in a bunker along with a Japanese soldier.

The Comfort Girls

Kim was a "comfort girl" and looked the part in an above-the-knee length dress that was obviously all she was wearing. We put MP guards around her and Sgt. Karl Yoneda of the OWI asked me if he could ask her a few questions. Since we were overwhelmed with legitimate POWs to question, I said yes. I never did learn what Karl asked her or what she answered. I asked her a few routine questions later, but it was readily apparent that she had no valuable information. The next day we put her on a plane for Ledo to be turned over to the British who were responsible for all POWs and civilians.

There are no official records of the Korean comfort girls. No one knows how many of these unfortunate young women were forced into prostitution by the Imperial Japanese forces during World War II. Estimates run as high as 200,000. Mostly daughters of Korean farmers and peasants—although some came from the city slums and some may have practiced the oldest profession previously—between 1935 and 1945 they were rounded up by the Kempei Tai and sent to China, Burma, Guam, Malaya, the Philippines, the Dutch East Indies, in fact anywhere in the vast Pacific theatre of war where Japanese troops were garrisoned. Thousands were killed during the bloody fighting in the Pacific, Southeast Asia, and elsewhere. Following the Japanese surrender, many were repatriated by the Allies, eventually returning to Korea. The Japanese destroyed all records of this chapter in the history of the Imperial forces. Only a few photos remain today.

The comfort girls were organized by the Japanese into what they euphemistically called the Women's Volunteer Labor Corps. They were grouped down to platoon level of about fifty girls each. Some were exclusively for the pleasure of Japanese officers. Others serviced NCOs while the least attractive were forced to cater to the lowly private soldier of the Emperor. Each platoon-sized group was commanded by a Mama-san, usually a middle-aged Japanese woman who spoke Korean. When the girls weren't engaged in their primary occupational specialty or were ill, they acted as the washerwomen and barracks maids in the troop rest areas.

No one knows what has become of those who survived the war.

Most would be in their early or mid-sixties today. United Nations troops in Korea between 1950 and 1953 reported that some of the girls continued to practice the profession after returning to Korea. Some also did that on Okinawa. For the vast majority, however, the stigma and shame resulting from what they had been forced to do prevents research and the absence of official records leaves one to conjecture as to the fate of those still living.

The 18th and 56th Imperial Japanese Army divisions in northern Burma each apparently had a platoon of comfort girls attached. Most were kept in the headquarters areas, principally in Myitkyina and Bhamo. When Myitkyina fell on 3 August 1944, some twenty-one of the girls were still there. How many had attempted to raft down the Irrawaddy could not be determined. Undoubtedly, many who tried were killed by Allied marksmen from the river banks along with the fleeing Japanese troops. Others probably died from starvation and exposure in the jungles of north Burma. About a week after Kim was picked up, processed, and sent back to Ledo, twenty more of the girls either turned themselves in or were picked up by our forces. In various stages of dress and undress, they could have caused a small riot among both Chinese and American troops who hadn't seen a female in quite some time. However, a quick-thinking American military police officer immediately segregated them from the male prisoners, found clothing that more adequately covered them and got them into tents inside a guarded barbed-wire enclosure, where they were protected from victor and vanquished alike.

At about 0930 hours on 8 August, Sgt. Grant Hirabayashi, an interpreter-translator with the 5307th came to see me. (When Ichimura and Koike had been recalled to NCAC headquarters, we'd been able to get help from some of the Nisei assigned to Merrill's Marauders.) "Captain," he said, "you aren't gonna believe this, but I've got about twenty female, I think Korean, POWs down at the center and I need help." Along with sergeants Howard Furumoto and Robert Honda, Grant and I went down to the improvised female POW processing point. A GI MP guard opened the gate and let us enter. Inside a large British style tent with the sides rolled up because of the heat were the female prisoners. They were dressed for the most part in ill-fitting, shapeless, and not very clean dresses or baggy pants and blouses. They were sitting or squatting on makeshift mats. An elderly Japanese Mama-san in the traditional Japanese kimono was with them. The

girls were young, eighteen to twenty-four was my guess. Some, despite their makeshift clothing and lack of even rudimentary grooming,
were still attractive. Their expressions varied. One or two appeared
defiant, but most wore looks of fear and anxiety. Some obviously had
tears in their eyes or running down their cheeks while some with their
heads bowed low appeared to be praying. None exhibited the coquetry
usually attributed to camp followers. I'd heard the stories of female
prostitutes serving with the Japanese and had only half believed them.
But here they were. Could they have any intelligence information that
would be of help to us? After all, it is said that a man is most vul-
nerable during the act of love. I was anxious to obtain some valuable
intelligence since so far at least the low-ranking soldiers I had interrogated hadn't provided much.

I had with me a number of photographs of Japanese officers who
were supposed to be commanders of units of the 18th and 56th divisions that I showed to the girls, which Grant asked them to identify
in his fluent Japanese. The girls (Koreans all) spoke some Japanese,
but it was of the bedroom and kitchen variety and extremely limited.
When you added that to their confusion, fear, and general lack of
education, the answers they gave weren't worth much. They mum-
bled in a mish-mash of Korean and Japanese in answer to the questions, but one of them did finally identify a photo of Colonel Maruyama as commander of the 114th Regiment. (I got the impression
that the young woman who made the identification had known the
good Colonel Maruyama very well indeed!)

Aside from that we got nothing of value. We had reached an im-
passe with the girls looking at us and us looking at them. After some
hesitation, one of the girls spoke to the Mama-san and the next thing
we knew all the girls were chattering hysterically. The old Mama-san
listened and then told the girls to be quiet. She looked at all four of
us and then approached me. (She obviously recognized rank when
she saw it.) She looked around again, and this time included Grant
in her look. (She also obviously recognized who spoke the best Japanese in the group.) Then, looking at me she spoke to Grant. She
asked if the girls could be permitted to know their fate. I instructed
Grant to tell her that confinement was only temporary. That just as
soon as possible they would be sent to India (I doubted if any of them
knew where India was) and eventually back to Korea. Grant spoke
in his best Japanese. The Mama-san translated to Korean.

The girls seemed to relax a bit, gave us a few tentative smiles, and directed more questions to Mama-san. She turned back to us. She said that she was responsible for the girls. She hesitated as if at a loss for words and squirmed a bit. Both Grant and I noticed that her obi, the traditional sash worn by all Japanese women, seemed a bit too full for her very small figure. It looked almost as if she were pregnant, which in view of her age didn't seem possible. I whispered a few words to Grant. He scuffed his feet a few times and then, as if he were talking to his mother or his aunt asked her if by any chance she might be hiding something. She smiled at Grant's obvious discomfort.

Nodding her head, she slowly began to unwind the voluminous obi and explained that being responsible for the girls also meant being responsible for their earnings. As members of the Women's Volunteer Corps they had been paid and had also received tips. When the Japanese fled Myitkyina, Mama-san had collected all the girls' money and kept it safe on her person. Grant was relieved and told the old lady "No problem." If money was all she had in the obi, both she and the girls would be able to keep what they had earned. She removed the obi and took from it neatly wrapped bundles of paper currency that she placed on the ground in front of us. The girls, whose knowledge of Japanese was not up to the task of understanding the exchange between Mama-san and Grant, watched anxiously.

Grant and I each picked up a bundle of the money. The bills were each for ten rupees and were still warm—either from Mama-san's body heat or from being hot off the press—they were Japanese occupation scrip. Something like our own scrip used in Europe and Asia, it was a paper promise by the Japanese government to pay by some unspecified date the amount of ten Burmese rupees. With the loss of northern Burma and what appeared to be the eventual total defeat of the Imperial forces, the scrip was undoubtedly worthless. Grant and I slowly placed the bundles back on the ground in front of Mama-san. Grant looked at me and I nodded my agreement to what I knew he was thinking. He looked at the girls, shrugged, and then as gently as he could explained to the old lady that what she had was money printed by the Japanese and now that the Japanese had been defeated, the money was worthless, had no value.

Mama-san looked at us in total disbelief. Her mouth opened but no sound came out. She pointed to the money on the ground, looked at us questioningly, and shook her head back and forth. Slowly she stooped over and picked up the bundles of paper money. Very carefully she replaced them in the obi and very slowly rewound it around her waist. For some reason it didn't look as full as it had a few minutes before. After talking with me, Grant turned back to the Mamasan and asked her for one or two of the bundles. He explained we could probably exchange the scrip for cigarettes, candy, and food with American and Chinese souvenir hunters. Mama-san thought this proposition over for a few minutes. Then she slowly unwound the obi again, carefully removed two bundles of the scrip, and gave them to Grant. There was a collective sigh of relief from the girls. I'm certain they thought this exchange was the American version of the Oriental custom of "squeeze" and that the rest of their hard-earned money was now safe. Mama-san explained the whole caper to her girls. Some laughed, some cried, and when I thought of what these girls had endured to earn this worthless scrip I was heartsick.

Grant and I then interrogated the girls again. They were relaxed now, less fearful, and more willing to talk. But they really didn't know anything, at least not anything of military-intelligence value. They had no understanding of military operations. They were not courtesans or Mata Haris, and if any of their bed partners had revealed anything, it had meant nothing to them. Taken forcibly for the most part from their families farms and homes in far-off Korea, they were there only for the pleasure of the Imperial Japanese troops. As soon as transportation could be arranged, they were turned over to British custody in India. The Allied press made a big thing of the comfort girls in sensational releases. But I felt only sorrow for them.

The night before the girls left for India it became our turn to comfort the comfort girls. Grant, Howard, and Bob visited them for the last time. This time, instead of interrogations, we held a sing-along. Three Japanese-American GIs, one with a guitar, sang American, Japanese, and Hawaiian songs while the girls in turn sang "Airiang," the Korean love song, to the boys.

The MISLS at Camp Savage trained many Nisei who served gallantly with United States and Allied combat forces in Burma, in particular with the 5307th Comp Unit Prov (Merrill's Marauders), the 475th Infantry and the 124th Cavalry, the British 36th Division. I knew a few of these men and have covered some of their exploits. But the full story of this outstanding group of Japanese Americans would fill a book. America owes them her gratitude for their loyalty and devotion.

Post-Myitkyina, for the Record

On 29 July Colonel Stilwell visited MTF headquarters and had a long talk with me. He requested that I stay on another year in the CBI following a thirty-day leave at home. He said I was one of only two officers here who knew the enemy situation well. He went on to say that the rotation policy was no assurance that I would stay in the states long, and that if I were sent to another overseas theater I'd have to start from the bottom up. However, if I came back here after thirty-days' leave, it would look good on my record and he intimated he could then put me in for promotion to major. I told Colonel Stilwell, respectfully of course, that I would not volunteer for another year in the jungles of Burma. I'd been there over twenty months with no leave; I was tired mentally and physically and needed a change; I preferred to complete my two years and take my chances with rotation. I qualified all this by saying that if there was to be an emergency, it would be a different matter. He didn't appear to like my refusal, but he accepted it. Later that evening I wrote home giving the gist of what was said and concluding with:

> I'm looking into the possibilities of an assignment in Washington when my two years are up. I've seen enough here and been through a lot. I just want to get back to the states.

In the aftermath of the battle for Myitkyina, I think it important to put the record straight once and for all regarding the Japanese troop strength in the Myitkyina area during May, June, and July of 1944.

In volume II of their official history of the CBI, Romanus and Sunderland are critical of the MTF intelligence effort. They write that "after a period of uncertainty G-2 of the MTF set the number of Japs in the Myitkyina area on 15 June at 500, a gross underestimate."

It is true that the figure of 500 was reported by the 5307th on 15 June 1944 and was relayed by the MTF G-2 to NCAC, but this was done in a roundup. A G-2 roundup is merely a roundup of unevaluated information as received in G-2 from frontline units. It is not an intelligence estimate. Because of combat conditions, our units and/

or informants reported to us by the areas in which they were located and our G-2 roundup was broken down to reflect this input—Myitkyina, Sitapur, Maingna, Waingmaw, Bhamo Road, Sumprabum Road, Mogaung Railroad, etc. No attempt was made by the MTF G-2 to collate or verify this unevaluated information. There just was not time nor did we have the people to do it. That was the task of the G-2 at NCAC.

Consequently, care should be taken in citing figures from a roundup. The 5307th report of 500 Japanese reflected what they estimated was to their immediate front, not what may have been in the entire Myitkyina area. It should also be remembered that the Japanese did not concentrate their troops in the confined area at the bend of the Irrawaddy River known as Myitkyina where our airpower was blasting them daily.

If the postwar historians had added up the total of all the roundups for all the various areas around Mitch, they would have found that our estimate was mighty close to what the Japanese commanders reported postwar.

By 25 July the Japanese situation in Myitkyina was desperate and they were making arrangements to leave by whatever means possible. General Mizukami, infantry commander at Myitkyina, had committed suicide and Colonel Maruyama, the ranking officer, had left for Bhamo with a few hundred troops.

Before I left Shaduzup for Myitkyina on 12 June 1944, we on the G-2 NCAC staff felt that the enemy had roughly 3,000 effectives in the Myitkyina area because: (1) the Japanese command had had about a month's time to bring outlying troops into the area; (2) under interrogation a POW taken near Myitkyina on 8 June told me that between 2,000 and 2,500 troops were defending the area; (3) we knew that elements of the 114th Regiment that had been detached for fighting near Moguang had returned to their parent regiment in Myitkyina. Our estimates, given from time to time directly to the MTF commander, may not have been one hundred percent accurate—no estimate ever is—but when compared to postwar accounts by Japanese commanders who were there, they didn't miss by much. Incidently, our estimate of 4,075 Japanese killed by the Allies at Myitkyina also agreed with the Japanese commander's reports.

There was a lot of mopping up to do in the Myitkyina area. The Haswell Force from Fort Hertz in the north cleared out Maingna while the Chinese 42nd Regiment did the same for the area from Waingmaw to Myitkyina. The Chinese 50th Division crossed the Irrawaddy, cleared out Naugtalaw Island, and policed its former battle area. The Marauders were reorganized as the 475th Infantry Regiment and assigned to the 5332nd Brigade along with the 124th Cavalry Regiment (dismounted) formerly of the Texas National Guard, which didn't arrive at Myitkyina until the end of September. The Brigade, later called the Mars Task Force, also had the Chinese 1st Regiment (separate) and an assortment of support units. This force went into a training and bivouac area north of Mankrin. The 209th and 236th Engineer combat battalions were finally flown out of the Myitkyina area and back to Ledo where, after a period of R & R, they went back to being engineers once again.

As officer-in-charge of the POW interrogation point and document processing center, Myitkyina Airstrip, I found myself still working a twenty-four-hour day. Prisoners were being turned in (some voluntarily surrendered) in large numbers, almost 200 in all by mid-August. The Chinese and American units were bringing in from ten to fifteen a day. Nearly all required immediate medical attention. Most of the wounded had not had their dressings changed for days, if ever. The bandages were filthy, bloody rags while many had open, untreated wounds crawling with white maggots. There was no way these POWs could be adequately treated at Myitkyina, so I arranged for their rapid evacuation to the 20th General Hospital at Ledo. Howard Furumoto, Grant Hirabayashi, and Bob Honda, all from the Marauders, helped me complete and record pertinent information on each POW who was then tagged before being sent back. I figured that someone could question them in greater detail later on—probably me! Most of the prisoners were from the 114th Regiment, 18th Division, and the 148th Regiment, 56th Division, with a scattering from the 18th Mountain Battalion, 18th Division Artillery, 15th Airfield Battalion, and one or two from the 55th and 56th regiments. This confirmed but did not change the order of battle lists we'd already developed.

We segregated the few officers, non-commissioned officers, and code clerks, had the medics check them first, and then did a fast interrogation before sending them on to the 20th General. All the POWs seemed surprised at the humane treatment they got from the Americans. Ranking officers had told them they would be executed if they were captured by or surrendered to the Allies.

One wounded PFC carried a phonograph record wrapped in a dirty rag, his most prized and, I guess, his only possession. It was a recording of the most popular Japanese soldier song of the 1940s, *"Shina No Yoru"* (China Nights). Like "Waltzing Matilda" or "Lili Marlene," it was something of a theme song for the Japanese GI. This record had been brought from Japan in 1942 and the soldier had carried it through Malaya and Singapore, and through Burma from Rangoon to Myitkyina—unbroken—for a good two years. I think he regarded it as a good luck charm and it very well might have been, since he was still alive and now the war was over for him. We found no trace of the ranking officers of the Myitkyina garrison. POWs stated that Maruyama had left Myitkyina for Bhamo with most of the ablebodied defenders about four days before the town fell. Nobody would admit to knowing what had happened to General Mizukami. He had committed suicide after giving the order to surrender Myitkyina. Documents were collected, given a quick scan, and then stored. We just didn't have the time or personnel to fully translate and evaluate them. When the boys from NCAC got to Mitch, the job would be all theirs.

I took a break from the POW business one day and along with Major Wright, jeeped down to the refugee camp at Pamati. Here the British were housing, feeding, and caring for some 7,000 civilians: men, women, and children. Most were either Burmese or Indian with maybe fifty or so Anglo-Burmese or Anglo-Indian, and about 275 Chinese—some of whom spoke the Cantonese dialect so I felt right at home with them. The Burmese were townspeople made homeless by the destruction of Myitkyina. The Indians were either civil servants of the British-Burmese government who had not gotten out before the Japanese came in or merchants who saw a profit and didn't want to get out. The fifty or so Anglo-Indians and Anglo-Burmese faced the most uncertain future. Products usually of an English soldier or civil servant and an Indian or Burmese woman, they had a place as long as the empire survived, but the British wouldn't accept them into English society and the Indians and Burmese despised them as bastards or worse. The overseas Chinese who had settled in Myitkyina were typical of their genre. Entrepreneurs, merchants, restaurateurs, they made a rupee any way they could—and they usually could—by dealing with friend and foe alike. However, as the fighting got hotter and hotter in Mitch the Japanese impressed the males, put them in uniform, gave them rifles, and put them on the outer defense perimeter. Their families were held as hostages to ensure their good behavior.

It was a well-run camp, with a British major named Haines, a civil affairs officer, in charge, who reported to General Wessels of the U.S. Army. The Americans provided medical supplies and equipment, but the Brits did the rest. It looked as though they would be doing it for quite some time given the almost total destruction of Myitkyina.

While Major Wright talked with Haines, I spent my time in the Chinese part of the camp listening to the stories of Burma and the hardships of the Myitkyina siege. The story that one old man told intrigued me. He had been born in Burma, an overseas Chinese, and had lived there all his life as had his father before him. He said the Chinese had been in Burma for more than a hundred years and the jade was discovered in Burma by the Chinese. He himself had been a buyer of jade and had traveled to the jade mines of north Burma each year for many years. Recently, however, bandits and other problems forced him and the other Chinese buyers to stay in towns like Mogaung and Myitkyina, where they would set up shop when the spring monsoon was finished and buy jade brought to them by the natives or by salesmen from the mines. After the Japanese came, no buyers could go north and all trading was done this way. He and his associates would grade and buy jade in large chunks. They would cut the jade so as to fit into small and inconspicuous packets and following age-old trade routes smuggle it out of Burma by way of Bhamo northeast to Yunnan Fu in China.

We completed our initial interrogation of the POWs on 17 August 1944. That same day the Myitkyina Task Force closed at the airstrip. I flew back to Ledo to take over the G-2 desk and to take on the job of further questioning the POWs we'd sent there from Mitch! Just before I left, General Wessels asked G-2 to give him an estimate of the total number of Japanese killed during the battle for Myitkyina. As the Japanese specialist, my estimate to Major Wright was 4,075. I noted later that Gen. Tanaka Shinichi and Col. Fusayasu Maruyama gave about the same figure in their postwar interrogations.

PART IV
AFTERMATH

The 20th General Hospital

The 20th General Hospital at Ledo was commanded by Colonel Isador Ravdin. The unit had arrived in Ledo in late March of 1943. The monsoons of 1943 were particularly bad and in those early months the hospital struggled through primitive conditions. The American nurses of the 20th were indeed to be commended for the cheerful, uncomplaining way in which they accepted the rigors of CBI duty: the climate, snakes, lizards, mosquitos and other insects, not to mention the occasional wild animals that wandered through their living compound. For the first few months the hospital wards were large tents that frequently leaked during the torrential rains; the floors were of hard-packed dirt; the nurses bathed under makeshift showers made from fifty-five-gallon drums; their clothes never got completely dry, but they made the best of it.

The hospital took care of American and Chinese soldiers as well as troops of other nationalities fighting in Burma or working on the Stilwell Road. Colonel Ravdin set up a separate compound to house and care for the wounded and ill Japanese POWs. How many POWs were there? Dr. John Paul North, then chief of surgery at the 20th General, wrote in the magazine *Surgery,* October 1964:

> Sick and wounded Japanese prisoners to the number of 312 were admitted, confined, and treated within the POW area. Many were desperately ill with malaria, dysentery, beriberi, and internal parasites. 132 of these had received no prior surgical care whatsoever.

The female nurses at the 20th did not work on the POW wards. Male corpsmen looked after the prisoners. However, these women were a tough bunch and I know that they would have done so if asked. I met a number of these fine young American women, like Grace Kindig and Jane Hassler, and when it turned out that one of them, Lorraine Craig, and I shared a birthday on 7 September, the Chih Hui Pu staff threw a party for us at a small Chinese restaurant in Ledo.

Special Order #218 dated 5 August 1944 USAAF, CBI, APO

885 finally reached me. The order extended my flight duties from 1 July 1944 to 30 June 1945. Maybe I would draw flight pay yet, although I hadn't planned on still being in the CBI in June 1945!

Meanwhile, the POW compound at the 20th General was bulging at the seams with Mizukami's veterans from Myitkyina. A special ID card issued by NCAC and controlled by G-2 allowed only the 20th General corpsmen, the doctors, me and my staff, and a few others on proven official business to get past the eagle-eyed MPs and into the prisoner area. As far as I know, no POW ever escaped from the 20th General and frankly, I doubt that many tried to do so. Why should they? They were housed, fed, clothed, and medically treated better than they had been for over two years; and since by the code of Bushido they were legally dead anyway and couldn't go home, they were better off here.

I ran a one-man show from 18 August until mid-September, no interpreter-translators or administrative help. To keep from getting completely swamped, I decided to use some of the local talent available in the POW hospital compound. I first selected a Japanese lieutenant who had some background in personnel matters. Then between us we selected six NCOs with varying degrees of administrative skills. All had at least a rudimentary knowledge of English. This little group became my POW personnel section. I drew up a form that had spaces for entering each prisoner's name, rank, unit, place and date of birth, control number, military-civilian job skills, and languages spoken. Using this information we prepared a master roster both in English and Japanese of all POWs at the hospital. It became a most useful interrogation tool for me and later for Staff Sergeants Roy Hiramatsu and Hedeo Makino who were assigned to Ledo by Colonel Stilwell about 16 September. Both had been at the headquarters in New Delhi and welcomed a transfer to Ledo. The master roster proved also to be a very useful tool for the administrators at the 20th General.

It was difficult to reconcile the dirty, unshaven, hollow-eyed, sunken-cheeked, emaciated men I had briefly interrogated at Myitkyina during the first two weeks in August with the ones that faced me today. The POWs of August had been dressed in rags, many were wounded, and all were ill. They were sullen, uncommunicative, and had that hopeless look of men who know they're about to die. I had requested that they be assembled in groups of twenty—the ambulatory ones, that is—in a dayroomlike structure in the POW compound.

When I entered the room, the first group had already been assembled and to a man they rose to their feet and stood at attention. Those from Myitkyina appeared to recognize me although I could not reciprocate. Two weeks of GI food three times a day was already showing its effect. All were clean shaven, had haircuts, and were wearing clean clothes on clean bodies. In my best Japanese I told them to be at ease. They smiled and relaxed a bit. One lieutenant had apparently been designated as their spokesman. He stepped forward, bowed low, and spoke in a soft Japanese:

> We are grateful to our captors. When we suffered the final ig-
> nominy of defeat coupled with capture or surrender, we believed
> that our lives had come to an end. We had been told by our
> superiors and we believed that you would first torture us to ob-
> tain information and then kill us. Instead, you have treated us
> with compassion and as human beings. You have cleansed our
> wounds, cured our illnesses; you have fed us, clothed us, pro-
> vided us with a bed, a place to wash, with life itself. You must
> know that we can never return to Japan. To do so would disgrace
> our families—would shame them and our ancestors. To our fam-
> ilies we are dead men and must so remain. As to our future, we
> will discuss that in time. As for now, ask us what you will and
> we will do our best to answer you truthfully.

The lieutenant again bowed low, then stepped back. The group bowed low in unison. It was a moving experience.

Initial questioning was aimed toward obtaining intelligence that would be of tactical value to the planners and participants in the forth-coming Third Burma campaign. I figured that the detailed, strategic, long-range interrogating could be done later at the Red Fort Prison in New Delhi where the prisoners would be taken when released from the 20th General. We didn't get too much out of our interrogations despite the fact that all the POWs were both cooperative and talkative. They just didn't know much of an intelligence value. Much to my surprise I did learn that most of them had been trying to get into, not out of, Myitkyina when captured, even as late as mid-July. They had come from north of the town by raft or road. Very few made it all the way to Mitch, which spoke well for our side. One prisoner I ques-tioned in a bit more detail had been part of a company of about 150

who had made it from Pidaung on the trace of the Mogaung-Myitkyina Railroad all the way to Sitapur north of Myitkyina about mid-
June. I'd been wandering around that area at that time, alone! As I've
said many times, the good Lord was protecting me!

It was hard to believe but a number of the prisoners, knowing that
they couldn't go home to Japan, expressed a desire to go to the United
States! I thought of our relocation centers for Japanese Americans and
what I knew to be the feeling of most Americans, especially those
who had husbands, brothers, fathers, sons, or daughters serving here
and in the Pacific, and then I suggested to them that they had better
look elsewhere, maybe South America.

With Sergeants Hiramatsu and Makino on board, I felt that I could
afford to take some leave. I'd had none since arriving in the CBI
theater over twenty-one months earlier and I felt ready for a break.
I got one. Colonel Stilwell authorized me fifteen-days leave, which
I spent in New Delhi.

While on leave in Delhi, John K. Emmerson filled me in regarding a group of prisoners turned in at Myitkyina. It seems that they
were captured by Sgt. Kenji "Kenny" Yasui, a Nisei, and others during mop-up operations following the fall of the town—a feat for which
Kenji was later decorated.

I got back to Ledo just in time to line up for a series of booster
shots—smallpox, typhoid, cholera, typhus—all given concurrently
and boy did they create a reaction! I was miserable that night and
most of the next two days.

It was tough to get back in the groove at Ledo, but I managed.
The Third Burma campaign was about to begin and NCAC at Ledo
was up to its collective armpits in the planning.

We'd come a long way from the days of Ramgarh, Margherita,
Mile Mark 5 1/2, Ledo, Shingbwiyang, Myitkyina. From one good
and one fair Chinese division; from 3,000 Americans that made up
the Marauders; from a ragtag, bobtailed outfit commanded by a feisty,
acerbic American general with wire-rimmed glasses, a GI crew cut,
and canvas leggins of another era, who hated pomp and circumstance.
We now had not one but two well-trained Chinese armies, the new
First Army commanded by Sun Li-jen, which had the 30th and 38th
divisions, veterans of the Hukawng Valley and the Myitkyina campaigns, and the new Sixth Army commanded by Gen. Liao Yao-hsiang,
who had commanded the 22nd Division and incurred Stilwell's wrath
when he refused to attack. He apparently was back in the good graces

of both Chiang Kai-shek and Stilwell. The new Sixth had the 14th, 22nd, and 50th divisions, all combat tested to one degree or another. The old and new Marauders had been reorganized into the 475th Infantry Regiment (LRP) and with the 124th Cavalry Regiment (dismounted), and the Chinese 1st Regiment (sep) formed into the 5332nd Brigade (prov) commanded by Brig. Gen. John P. Willey and called the Mars Task Force. On the west General Stilwell had the British-Indian 36th Division. All in all, a formidable combat force that with all the support troop units must have numbered about 100,000 men (and a few women).

The Japanese were reeling from their defeats at Myitkyina and Imphal and the continual pounding they were getting from the bombers of the 10th USAAF. They still had three field armies in Burma—the fifteenth, twenty-eighth and thirty-third—with a total of ten divisions, but all the divisions were under strength and strung out from Rangoon to Bhamo on the south-north axis and from the Salween to the Railroad Corridor on the east-west line. It seemed we would be able to clear Burma of the Japanese in this campaign.

Colonel Stilwell again asked me to consider taking a thirty-day leave stateside and returning to the CBI. If I had honestly thought I was indispensable, I might have considered it, but I wasn't. I was tired after two years in the CBI and I thought it was time to rotate.

On 21 October 1944 word filtered down from Myitkyina that General Stilwell had been relieved of command and recalled to Washington. This news hit like a bombshell at Ledo headquarters. Why? What had happened? Was he ill? No one could conceive of the relief and recall of a general who had just won a brilliant victory against all odds in the jungles of north Burma during the monsoons. I did not learn the truth until years later and I doubt if many Americans know, or, for that matter, really care today. Stilwell was a patriot, a proud man who practiced for forty-six years the tenets of duty, honor, and country. He served briefly in the Pacific under MacArthur in 1945 and then took command of the United States Sixth Army at the Presidio of San Francisco where he died on 12 October 1946 just two years following his relief of command—a great soldier and a great American.

Third Burma Campaign

The Third Burma campaign, which was to culminate in the total defeat of the Japanese in Burma, began on or about 14 October 1944, just one week before General Stilwell's relief and recall. At Ledo I now had a staff of five in the G-2 section (including myself). Staff Sergeants Hiramatsu and Makino had been augmented by T-5s Arthur Thomas and Alvin Halprin. We were whittling away at the backlog of POWs at the 20th General and were preparing to receive more prisoners from the Allied forces. They weren't long in coming. The British 36th Division, the new Chinese First and Sixth armies, and the 5332nd U.S. Brigade (Mars Task Force) all advanced steadily southward and southeastward. The rank of the new prisoners, their reports of low morale and shortages of all kinds of supplies, told us that the Japanese in Burma were on the run. Without exception the prisoners, from private to lieutenant, were talkative and cooperative. Most had been in and out of combat since Singapore in early 1942, although there was a scattering of raw recruit replacements straight from Japan. All seemed glad to be out of it alive.

POWs were spot interrogated by G-2 Forward at Myitkyina as I had done immediately after the fall of that town. Those that were in need of immediate medical attention were sent to the 20th General where we continued the interrogation after which the boys of the OWI did a psychological profile. Later the POWs were sent to the permanent prisoner facility at the Red Fort in New Delhi where they were given a complete and more fully detailed work-up.

Much has been said and written about the Japanese POW. He would never voluntarily surrender; he would face death before dishonor, commit suicide before allowing himself to be captured; if unable to avoid capture because of wounds or illness, he would never talk and would try to kill himself at the first opportunity. Not necessarily so.

In my experience with Japanese POWs, which began with the first one, captured by the Chinese, I interrogated back in the Hukawng Valley in December 1943 to those I interrogated at Myitkyina in August 1944 and at Ledo and the 20th General Hospital after that, I found a wide variance in the responses of POWs. True, the Japanese soldier (sailor, marine, airman) was taught the "Code of Bushido"— Code of the Warrior, and was expected to live and die by it. But, like our own orders to give only name, rank and serial number, some did and some did not, depending on the individual. Three examples stand out in my mind.

On 25 October 1944 the British 36th Division, operating in the

Railroad Corridor, captured a Pfc who said he was an ammo carrier with the 128th Regiment, 53rd Division. Later, near Kuktaw, they picked up a superior private who said he had belonged to the 151st Regiment, 53rd Division, which he told us had retreated from the Imphal debacle.

Three Japanese were captured by Detachment 101 Kachins near Mansi in late September 1944, a lieutenant and two enlisted men. All talked freely. The lieutenant was an artilleryman with the 18th Division. He said he had participated in the Hukawng Valley actions and with the enlisted men was searching for two of the unit's pack elephants that had strayed away while the unit was retreating toward Namhkam. The lieutenant also told us of the Japanese defeat at Taihpa-Ga and the retreat south to Kamaing. One of the enlisted men, a superior private, was a seasoned veteran. He had been with the 56th Regiment from the capture of Singapore through the conquest of Burma and the Hukawng Valley campaigns.

The Chinese, operating near Shwegu south of Myitkyina, on 4 November 1944, captured and turned over to us a Pfc who said he was a member of the 16th Regiment, 2nd Division. He told of a hospital unit he saw trying to make its way on foot to Namhkam with remnants of the 114th Regiment, 18th Division, from the battle of Myitkyina.

We didn't get too much new intelligence from these groups but we did get a wealth of information regarding order of battle and I was able to confirm a great deal of information that had been previously reported but not confirmed. Like all POWs, Japanese POWs talked, particularly when well treated.

By mid-November 1944, most of the NCAC staff had moved from Ledo to Myitkyina. Included was my bashamate of six months, Maj. Stu Crossman. He spoke Mandarin Chinese with a decided Yankee accent but still gave orders to our Chinese orderly, Yang, much better than I did. He got obedience! Stu loved Chinese food and would go with me to the Ledo Cantonese restaurant every chance he got. He requested that I ask the owner to permit him to watch the preparation of Chinese food and I gained much "face" when the owner agreed to do so. Later, during the Third Burma campaign while stationed at Bhamo, Stu began a short Chinese cookbook that he gave to his friends. When he finally retired from the Army and settled in Florida, he taught Chinese cooking!

Not many USO shows made it to the CBI and of those that did very few ever got to the forward areas. A notable exception was the Pat O'Brien-Jinx Falkenberg Show, which came to Ledo twice—once in July and again in November 1944—and to Myitkyina in December 1944. Pat and Jinx were a pair of real troupers, as were all the men and women with them. After the November performance I had the privilege of talking with Pat, a great guy, a real gentleman, and superb raconteur. He told humorous stories, one right after the other, never repeating himself, never using obscenities or anything off color.

Another myth I'd like to put to rest is that the Chinese have no mechanical ability. The Chinese units in Burma didn't have much in the way of vehicular support but the ones they did have always ran. They may not have looked good and I saw some real Rube Goldberg field expedients, but they ran.

On 9 November 1944 I saw my name on the March 1945 rotation list! Some of the guys on the January list left that same day so it was possible I could get out in January, a month over three years since I reported to Crissy Field at the Presidio of San Francisco. I'd just learned that the MISLS had moved to Fort Snelling, Minnesota.

The Third Burma campaign continued to go well. According to the 2 to 23 December 1944 situation report, the British 36th Division had the toughest going down the Railroad Corridor, but they kept slugging along. The new Chinese First Army under General Sun Li-jen took Bhamo and reached the Burma-China border while the Americans of the 5332nd Brigade (Mars) began a difficult cross-country forced march to cut the old Burma Road near Namhkam.

On 20 December 1944, these orders finally arrived:

1. Special Order #51 Extract. NCAC, APO 218, dated 16 Dec. '44. Capt. Won-loy Chan, 0345689, FA 9301M, is relieved from further assignment and duty . . . and is attached unassigned to REPL SV USF IBT.

2. Ltr. Order #41, dated 20 Dec. '44. Relieved from duty in IBT to an airport in the United States. Upon arrival report to the Debarkation Officer for further orders.

I said good-bye to the greatly reduced gang at Ledo and grabbed my last L-5 flight to Myitkyina. It seemed odd to go east to get out, but Mitch was now the big air terminal for eastern India and Burma.

I called on Colonel Stilwell for the last time and received from him some personal letters to deliver to his father, the general. I drove around the Myitkyina Airfield, now the site of a bustling NCAC headquarters, air base, and supply depot. Just six months ago it had been the site of the most crucial battle for north Burma!

I began the first leg of my flight home on 21 December 1944. Three old friends came down to see me off including Bill Toy, who had taught me to ride a motorcycle back at Ramgarh almost two years ago. I boarded a C-47 along with Majs. Ben Gearhart and Garnett Giesler and Lt. Fred Denman, all of whom had come with me to the CBI on the *Île de France*. The other passengers I didn't know. My last view of Mitch was from 3,000 feet—how peaceful it looked!

Rotation and Retrospections

From Mitch we flew to Lalaghat, refueled, and then went on to Karachi on India's northwest coast on the edge of the Sind Desert. We stayed at the old British 8th Army camp that was now an American SOS base. In a day or so it was off to Aden on the Gulf of Aden and then to Khartoum in the Sudan where Generals Kitchener and "Chinese" Gordon had carved out another piece of the British Empire almost fifty years ago. There we overnighted at a USAAF base. The next day we flew north to the coast of the Mediterranean Sea and then along the north rim of Africa with stops at Tripoli and Casablanca before turning southwest and landing at Accra on the Gold Coast. Here we switched from the twin-engine C-47 to a four-engine C-54 for the long hop across the Atlantic by way of Ascension Island, landing at Natal in Brazil some ten hours later. Another overnighter and then it was on to Miami by way of Georgetown, British Guiana, and San Juan, Puerto Rico. We landed at Miami on 2 January 1945— thirteen days from Myitkyina. It had taken me thirty-eight days to get to the CBI but only about one-third of that to get back!

But I wasn't home yet. The fun had just begun. Special Order #3, dated 3 January 1945, sent me on to Camp Beale, California, for reassignment. I reported to the USAAF desk at Miami that controlled all CONUS flights where I was told, "We're booked up for three weeks, Captain. Maybe you should get a car and drive to California or take a train." I checked the driving possibilities and then wired Ruby—"Can drive to San Francisco and be there by 11 Jan. Will phone you tonight."

At the Officer's Club that evening the response was "You mean you're taking on one of those delivery cars to the West Coast?" I said I was. "You'll be sorry. None of them are in good shape. The tires are retreads and if you blow one, there ain't no way to buy, beg, or steal another. Better take the train." I wired Ruby a second time, "Proceeding by train on 4 Jan. Should reach California in five days."

I was due to board a troop train headed for Camp Beale, California, at 5:00 P.M. on 4 January. At 3:00 P.M. the USAAF CONUS flight control desk phoned me, "Captain Chan, we got space for you on tomorrow's nonstop to Burbank, California. Can you make it?" Could I make it? Hell yes! I wired Ruby a third time, "Am flying instead. Should arrive Los Angeles 5 January. See you soon." I'm certain that by this time Ruby thought I'd completely lost my mind in Burma.

A C-47 got me to Burbank and a Greyhound bus got me from there to Tulare. My reporting date at Beale was 9 January so I stayed a couple of days at Tulare. Then I drove north to Carmel where General Stilwell had his home. He was away, but I left the letters from his son and drove on north to Camp Beale near Marysville, California. Two days later amended orders gave me three weeks leave plus ten days Rest and Recreation at the USAAF R & R Center in beautiful Santa Barbara, California. I headed down to San Francisco to visit with my relatives and then on to Tulare. Ruby and I drove to Las Vegas where we were married on 2 February 1945 and then immediately headed for Santa Barbara. The R & R at the Miramar Hotel was the time and place of our honeymoon and what a wonderful time it was. Forty years later we're still husband and wife.

On 11 February I learned that my next assignment was to be at the U.S. Army Field Artillery School, Fort Sill, Oklahoma. While my original 1936 commission had been in the field artillery, I had never served one day with the cannoneers nor had I ever fired a field-artillery piece. I knew the field-artillery song "The Caissons Go Rolling Along" and I'd sampled field artillery and French 75 punches at the Officers Clubs. That was the extent of my knowledge and experience. So be it. I was a field-artillery officer and personnel decided that I should finally perform as one.

I drove my new bride of fifteen days back to Tulare and caught the Greyhound for Lawton, Oklahoma and Fort Sill. The G-1 at Fort

Sill was no dummy, so instead of finding myself trying to teach artillery recruits—who probably knew as much as I did about the subject—I was assigned to the S-2 (intelligence) section at the Field Artillery Replacement Training Center Headquarters.

I'd just about settled in my new assignment the second week in March 1945, when General Stilwell, now commanding general of the U.S. Army Ground Forces, visited Fort Sill. The Fort Sill *Cannoneer* put it this way:

> STILWELL GREETS CHINESE FRIEND. "Gee, Chan, I'm glad to see you again." That was General Joseph W. Stilwell's greeting to Capt. Won-loy Chan, former intelligence officer on the general's staff during the Burmese campaign, now at the Field Artillery Replacement Training Center here. . . . Because of his work in intelligence, Capt. Chan is "Charlie" Chan to his fellow workers and even to General Stilwell. The American-born Chinese was graduated from Stanford University in 1936 and commissioned in the Field Artillery. Before going overseas in 1942 . . .

Actually, when General Stilwell greeted me he said, "Charlie, what the hell are you doing here?" I replied that I'd been ordered to Fort Sill by Army Ground Forces. "You don't belong here, Charlie," he said. A week later came a teletype from the adjutant general directing that I be sent to Washington, D.C., in connection with military-intelligence activities. After briefing the school troop officers at Fort Sill on intelligence in the CBI, I took off for Washington on 29 March with Ruby, who had driven to Sill from California. After reporting into the old Munitions Building, I was assigned to the Military Intelligence Division of the War Department and more specifically, to the Pacific Military Intelligence Research Section (PACMIRS) at Fort Ritchie, Maryland. Ruby found us a place to live nearby in Highfield, Maryland, and I settled down to being an intelligence "staff wallah" in the Washington area.

Later as I sat in my comfortable office at Fort Ritchie, nestled in the beautiful Catoctin Mountains of western Maryland, many things passed through my mind.

The Stilwell Road had been open since 28 January 1945 and supplies were flowing over it into the insatiable maw of China.

The war in Burma was almost over. The Mars Task Force had been airlifted into Kunming for combat duty in southwestern China. All Chinese combat units were on their way back home to continue fighting on Chinese soil. The British were consolidating their positions in Burma and reinstituting civil control.

I thought about Burma, the Burma I had known for almost two years. I thought about the Chinese soldier, the Ping. Up until Ramgarh in early 1943, he had been poorly equipped, rarely paid, ill fed, ill housed with little or no medical facilities, often mistreated by his superiors, and suffering from inadequate leadership. General Stilwell had said time and time again that with proper training, treatment, and leadership, the Chinese Ping would be the equal of any soldier in the world. At Ramgarh the general set out to prove it and prove it he did. Later in the fight for the Hukawng Valley and at the bloody siege of Myitkyina, I marveled at the endurance, intelligence, and bravery of the Ping. I watched him in victory and I watched him in defeat. I watched him in combat being killed or wounded. Many Chinese were decorated for bravery and commended by the U.S. military. One in particular that comes to my mind is Maj. Chao Yu-kan, who commanded the 3rd Battalion, 113th Regiment, 38th Division. He was awarded the U.S. Silver Star for valor resulting from action near Walawbum. He was later killed in action.

I thought of the Japanese soldier. He too was brave, intelligent, and possessed of almost superhuman endurance. He was bound by the Japanese warrior Code of Bushido: death with honor and loyalty, *gyokusai* (suicide) if it were impossible to win. A number of Japanese officers and some enlisted men chose this way at Myitkyina. Nevertheless, a large number of them were captured (most seriously ill or wounded), and when treated with a degree of kindness did talk. All said, however, that they were officially dead and could never go home.

I thought about the Asian American soldier in the CBI. It was doubly tough on us. For officers like Lt. James Chan and myself, operating and fighting in the jungles of north Burma was difficult indeed. The Chinese were our allies, right? The Japanese were our enemies, right? And the GIs of Merrill's Marauders were our buddies, right? Well, not necessarily so. To the Chinese we often resembled Japanese, while to the Japanese we often looked like Chinese. Japanese Americans had it even worse. Our Chinese allies tended to shoot first and ask questions later; the Japanese knew a Japanese American right away—he was well fed! The GIs—except those who worked directly with Japanese Americans—reacted like the Chinese. The Japanese American had the additional problem of coming to grips with the fact that back home his family was being held in detention centers. These men deserve the gratitude of all Americans. Without the presence of these MISLS-trained Japanese Americans in Burma and in the Pacific, winning World War II would have been much more difficult. I thought also of the discrimination, some subtle and some not so subtle, that still existed in the United States. Last but by no means least, I thought of my being here at Fort Ritchie in the spring of 1945. I thanked God for that eleventh-hour phone call right after Pearl Harbor that sent me to Crissy Field instead of Camp Roberts, for seeing me safely through twenty-three months in a combat zone and getting me back home in one piece while brave men next to me were killed or wounded, and for a man named Joseph W. Stilwell who came by Fort Sill when my career was apparently derailed and got it back on track.

For all these things I was humbled, my head was bowed. I uttered a prayer and thanked our Supreme Commander one more time.

I remained with the War Department Intelligence (WD-MID) and the Office of Naval Intelligence (ONI) until 1946. Then I was transferred to the newly established coordinating unit known as the Central Intelligence Group (CIG). I stayed with the CIG and other government agencies until my retirement twenty-seven years later. In 1968 at Fort Myer, Virginia, I retired with the rank of colonel from the United States Army.

APPENDIX

Interrogation of Lieutenant General Tanaka Shinichi, CG 18th Division

At the request of Maj. Gen. Orlando Ward, Chief of the U.S. Army Historical Division, Lieutenant General Tanaka was interrogated by the G-2 of the U.S. Army Far East Command in April 1949. Lieutenant General Tanaka had commanded the Japanese 18th Division in north Burma from March 1943 until the fall of Myitkyina in August 1944. From September 1944 until the final defeat of the Japanese forces in Burma in May 1945 he was Chief of Staff of the Japanese Burma-Area Army. His interrogation covered events from pre–Pearl Harbor to the conclusion of the Burma campaigns. What follows has been extracted from a voluminous collection of summaries, questions, and answers. It covers only those portions of the interrogation that are believed pertinent to *Burma: The Untold Story*. For students of the complete history of the war in Asia—the China-Burma-India Theater of Operations—the complete interrogation report is available from the National Records Center, Washington, D.C. 20408.

I. Fighting in the Hukawng Valley

A. Sharaw Ga, Ningbyen, Yubang Ga

Tanaka: In our initial clash with American and Chinese forces near the junction of the Tarung and Tanai rivers, I had only one company from the 2nd Bn., 56th Regiment, 18th Division—100 men with two heavy machine guns. It became clear to me after our first contact on 30–31 October 1943 that we were facing a strong Allied force advancing south from Ledo, India. We estimated that two divisions, 25,000 to 30,000 strong, would try to go through Shingbwiyang toward Maingkwan. In early November of 1943, I reinforced the company at Ningbyen with the balance of the 2nd Bn., 56th Regiment, 18th Division. This consisted of two infantry companies and one heavy machine gun company (400 men and six heavy machine guns).

B. Walawbum

Tanaka: While preparing for an offensive operation in the fall of 1943 at the right bank of the Tanai River against the expected advance of the American-Chinese forces from the direction of Shingbwiyang, I received an army order in November. It stated that the 18th Division would avoid a decisive battle on the Tanai River and intercept the enemy near Maingkwan. In any event the enemy must be checked north of Kamaing. In accordance with that order the division occupied a position in the Maingkwan area in late February 1944.

The attack did not make progress due primarily to the activity of enemy tanks and there were indications that the enemy was increasing his strength. Furthermore, I could not remain in contact with the 2nd Battalion of the 56th Regiment which was my right flank detachment and I felt that the division's right flank was in danger. In view of the fact that unified command of the division was difficult, I withdrew the division command elements on 7 March to the vicinity of Jambu Hkintang. My plan of operation was for the 18th Division to defend the Kamaing area to the end, so consequently a withdrawal from this area was not preplanned. I had been directed twice, in the summer and in November 1943, to hold the Kamaing area. I also received an order from the Burma army area commander in March 1944:

Henceforth a force with a nucleus of two infantry regiments will be placed under the command of the 18th Division commander and will attack the enemy in the Hukawng Sector. This is scheduled to be carried out in May 1944.

Due to the foregoing instructions and order, although I felt that I was encircled by superior American and Chinese forces at times, I did my best to secure the Kamaing area to the end; however I was finally compelled to withdraw at the end of June 1944 for the following reasons:

1. Since the operations in the Imphal area had failed, the scheduled offensive in the Hukawng was called off.

2. A six-month supply of ammunition and rations was to have been stocked in the Kamaing area and army headquarters was supposed to be responsible for transportation. Again due to Imphal, army could not do this and with railway transport cut off from early March to 10 May by the landing of enemy airborne raiding units in the Mawlu area the supply of ammunition, rations, and other supplies were almost exhausted.

Contrary to our expectations and intelligence reports the actions of the American and Chinese forces were intensive and vigorous and at times they displayed fighting power—their air superiority and air-supply capabilities were important. My division was almost completely encircled in the Kamaing area.

In May 1944 the operations of the American and Chinese forces greatly intensified. It may be that the approach of north Burma's monsoon season made them eager to proceed. At that time I took the following measure:

1. Against the Myitkyina offensive of the American and Chinese forces which commenced on or about 17 May I ordered Colonel Maruyama, commander of the Myitkyina garrison, to defend that area and at the same time dispatch two infantry battalions. [Author's note: Tanaka didn't say, or the interrogator didn't determine, to where or for what purpose the battalions were to be dispatched.] I sent Major Mihashi from the division G-2 to that area for liaison purposes. [Again, what area?] I decided it would be best to hold my present position until the end of May and then withdraw to prepared positions in Kamaing.

From intelligence received I felt it was imperative to delay construction of the Burma [Stilwell] Road as long as possible. In order to do this I felt that my division had to hold out in its present positions for at least three months—June, July, and August 1944. Efforts had to be made to hold Myitkyina because the rear of the 56th Division in the Yunnan [China] area would be open to the enemy if it were abandoned. It was also necessary if we were to support the flanks and rear of the Fifteenth Army which had failed in the Imphal operation. For both these reasons I considered it absolutely necessary to hold Kamaing and all my subsequent actions were predicated on this. Enemy operations became increasingly active in late May. In particular, enemy forces encircled the Maingkwan area to the upper reaches of the Tanai River basin. To counter this move, the right flank of my division [the 1st Battalion of the 55th Infantry Regiment] was ordered to check the enemy in the vicinity of the mountain area north of Kamaing. In addition the 146th Infantry Regiment of the 55th Division was also assigned to that area and both units were placed under MG Aida, my infantry group commander.

The monsoon season was considerably advanced by the latter part of May 1944. Traffic off the roads was confined to foot. The ration of rice was decreased to 100 grams per day per man [normally 860 grams]. There was no replenishment of ammunition and the use of shells was limited to four per gun per day. There was almost no gasoline. Malarial cases increased and all patients were suffering from malnutrition; the number of men in some companies decreased to about thirty with some numbering only fifteen. During this period we attacked with all the strength possible but we did not succeed. Less than 700 kilograms of supplies were supplied. The daily ration of rice decreased to 70 grams. There were many infantry companies whose strength decreased to less than ten.

C. Conclusions

Tanaka: The basic reason why the Japanese 18th Division was able to escape on both of these occasions is very simple. With the training given by the American military authorities the Chinese forces displayed splendid maneuverability, particularly when supported by U.S. supplies from the air. For this reason the Japanese were always outflanked. However, in units smaller than regiments the Chinese displayed shortcomings in their mutual support, reconnaissance ability, and in being able to devise independent measures to cope with changes in the situation. This created tactical gaps in the lines at various points which in turn made it possible for my forces to avoid envelopment and defeat by escaping through these gaps.

Interrogator: After your first clash with American-Chinese units on or about 30–31 October 1943 what estimate did you and your staff make of the situation?

Tanaka: We believed that these forces were endeavoring to advance south through Ledo. We estimated their strength to be approximately 100,000 troops [5 divisions plus mechanized units of the United States Army]. We also estimated that only two divisions—25,000–30,000 men—would lead the advance via Shingbwiyang toward Mainkwan. [Author's note: Stilwell had but two Chinese divisions plus the Chinese tank unit led by Col. Rothwell Brown and the Galahad Force (Merrill's Marauders) in Burma at that time—a total of not more than 50,000 of which perhaps 30,000 participated in the Hukawng Valley campaign. Thus it appears that while Tanaka's overall estimate of 100,000 was well off the mark his estimate of the force he faced was right on that mark.]

Tanaka (con't): I decided that the position of my forces at Ningbyen was untenable and would fall to the enemy since the main strength of my division [18th] was such a great distance from Ningbyen that it would have taken about one month for me to get reinforcements there. I developed a plan to advance the main body of the division to Shingbwiyang and destroy enemy forces that would be advancing through the mountains from the north. However Lt. Gen. Mutaguchi, commander of the Fifteenth Army did not approve and the plan was not implemented. General Mutaguchi was preparing for the Imphal offensive at the time and decided he would need all available transport, etc., for that operation making it difficult if not impossible to concurrently supply the 18th Division. Instead, in mid-December General Mutaguchi ordered me to fight a delaying action, which I proceeded to do.

II. The Siege of Myitkyina

Interrogator: What strength did you have for the defense of Myitkyina in the spring of 1944?

Tanaka: The 114th Regiment minus one battalion, about 2,500 to 3,000 troops. I ordered the 3rd Battalion to join the regiment in May following the attack on Myitkyina. We had built temporary field positions around the town but not fortified positions such as concrete pillboxes. Later I had another trench dug in the area east of Waingmaw near the Irrawaddy River. This was defended by some 200 troops. I also had temporary positions dug at Namti and at Punlumbum, each with company of troops.

Interrogator: What was your estimate of the size of the Allied force that attacked Myitkyina?

Tanaka: The American force we estimated at 3,000 men; the Chinese from the north we placed at division size [12,000], and the Chinese airborne unit flown in by the Americans also at division size; we estimated that the British had maybe 2,000 guerrillas in the mountains southwest of Myitkyina; a total Allied strength of approximately 30,000 or three divisions.

Interrogator: What was your supply situation at Myitkyina by early June 1944?

Tanaka: Very bad. It was impossible to bring in supplies from other areas because Myitkyina was blockaded by Allied forces. Supplies could not be flown in because we did not have the planes in Burma.

Also, what roads there were were in extremely bad condition because of the monsoons.

Interrogator: Did your garrison at Myitkyina ever attempt to break out thru the Allied lines?

Tanaka: We prepared a plan to do so but it was never carried out. It was to have been implemented on 30 May 1944 but orders from Lieutenant General Honda caused us to remain and defend Myitkyina. General Honda also said he was planning to reinforce our garrison with the 53rd Division by way of Moguang. [Author's note: This was not done and Moguang fell to the Allies before it could be reinforced.]

Interrogator: Was the garrison ever reinforced?

Tanaka: The 3rd Battalion rejoined the 114th in May, right after the initial Allied attack; sometime in June a battalion from the 56th Division at Bhamo managed to infiltrate into Myitkyina [with] 400 to 500 men. The garrison there suffered very heavy casualties and we wanted to hold the town as long as possible. In July Major General Mizukami from the 56th Division got thru with about thirty men. He had been sent by Lieutenant General Honda to replace Colonel Maruyama as commander of the garrison.

Interrogator: When were orders received to evacuate Myitkyina?

Tanaka: They were not "received," they were given by Major General Mizukami sometime in late July without reference to or approval by Lieutenant General Honda. Immediately after giving the order General Mizukami committed suicide.

Interrogator: Why do you think General Mizukami gave the order?

Tanaka: He knew that Lieutenant General Honda desired to hold Myitkyina at all costs but since elements of the 53rd Division did not reinforce the garrison as planned and no help was coming from the south it would have meant the annihilation of the entire Japanese garrison had they remained in Myitkyina defending against vastly superior Allied forces. To save what was left of his force from being wiped out he gave the order.

Interrogator: When did the evacuation begin and how was it carried out?

Tanaka: On or about 31 July 1944 with all movements carried out in darkness. Small groups floated down the Irrawaddy on rafts toward Bhamo. From a peak strength of 4,600 I do not believe that more than 600 escaped. The first small group left the town in early August.

GLOSSARY

A-2/3	An air force joint intelligence & operations section, usually attached to a ground force headquarters to work with the G-2/3 section.
A-36	A USAAF two-engine attack bomber.
Ack-Ack	Slang term for any automatic antiaircraft gun.
ALBACORE	Code name for Stilwell's plan to retake Burma. Plan was in three phases—Ledo to Myitkyina.
APO	Army Post Office. Used as a designator for all USA and USAAF units overseas during WW II.
AT Gun	Antitank gun.
B-25	USAAF four-engine bomber.
Banzai Charge	An all-out charge used by Japanese infantry.
Bn.	Battalion.
Basha	A native style hut favored by Burmese hill tribes and the natives of northeast India. Constructed of bamboo poles and leaves with rush or corrugated iron roofs.
Butai	Japanese term for Task Force.
Bum	Burmese for hill or mountain, e.g., Wantuk Bum.
C-46/47	USAAF two-engine cargo planes used in the CBI for the transport of troops and all classes of equipment and supply.
CIG	Central Intelligence Group.
Chih Hui Pu	Headquarters of the Chinese Army in India.
CAI	Chinese Army in India.
CBI	China-Burma-India Theater of Operations.
CMP	Chinese Military Police.

Chindits	British long-range penetration forces led by Brig. Orde Wingate. Name comes from the Burmese Chinthe, a mythological bird that guarded temples.
Chop	A personal seal, usually made of ivory, used by both Chinese and Japanese to authenticate documents.
CP	Command Post.
CONUS	Continental United States.
Div.	Division.
END RUN	Code name for Stilwell's plan to capture Myitkyina.
Fan-I-Kuan	Chinese interpreters assigned to U.S. advisors.
G-1	Personnel
G-2	Intelligence Used by divisions or higher.
G-3	Operations (Less than Division used "S".)
G-4	Logistics
GALAHAD	Code name for the combined U.S.-Chinese force that captured Myitkyina.
G-Mo	Generalissimo Chiang Kai-shek.
Hamp	Japanese aircraft of the Zero class.
Hka	River.
Hump	The India-China air ferry route.
IBT	India-Burma Theater of Operations. Came into being in October 1944.
ID	Identification card or number.
JICA	Joint Intelligence Collecting Agency.
Kanji(s)	Characters used in writing Chinese and Japanese.
Kempei Tai	Imperial Japanese Military Police.

KMT	Kuomintang. Originally the designation for Chiang Kai-shek's political party. Later used to designate Chinese military forces in southern China, north Burma, Laos and north Thailand.
L-4/5	USAAF light, single-engined aircraft.
LRP	Long range penetration units (U.S.).
LRPG	Long range penetration groups (British).
Mama-san	GI slang for middle-aged Japanese women.
MIS	U.S. Military Intelligence Service.
MISLS	U.S. Military Intelligence Service Language School.
MP	U.S. Military Police.
Mitch	GI slang for Myitkyina.
MTF	Myitkyina Task Force.
NCAC	U.S. Northern Combat Area Command.
Nisei	Second generation Japanese Americans.
NCO	U.S. Non-commissioned officer.
OB	Order of Battle. A compilation of enemy units and commanders with their believed locations.
ONI	U.S. Office of Naval Intelligence.
Oscar	Japanese aircraft of the Zero class.
OSS	U.S. Office of Strategic Services.
OWI	U.S. Office of War Information.
P-40/51	USAAF Fighter aircraft.
Ping	Chinese equivalent of the GI.
POW	Prisoner of War.
Psywar	Psychological warfare.
R & R	Rest & Recreation.

RECON or Recon	Reconnaissance.
Regt.	Regiment.
ROTC	Reserve Officers Training Corps.
Rupee	Unit of currency, India or Burma. Was at a ratio of 3 rupees to the U.S. dollar during WW II.
SEAC	Southeast Asia Command.
Shing	GI slang for Shingbwiyang.
SITREP	Situation Report.
SOS	U.S. Services of Supply.
TDY or Tdy.	Temporary duty.
TO&Es	Tables of Organization & Equipment.
Tojo	Japanese aircraft of the Zero class.
USA	United States Army.
USAAF	United States Army Air Force.
VIP	Very Important Person.
VOCG	Verbal order of the commanding general.
WD MID	War Department Military Intelligence Division.
Zeke	Japanese aircraft of the Zero class.

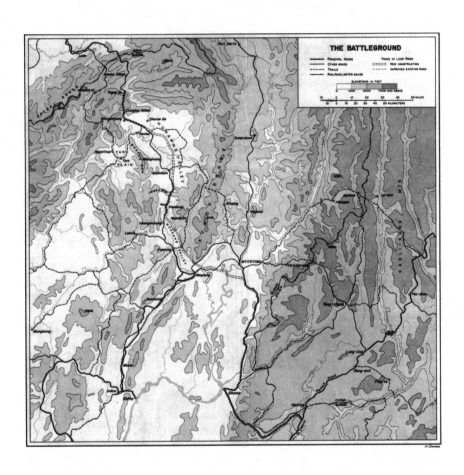

THE BATTLEGROUND

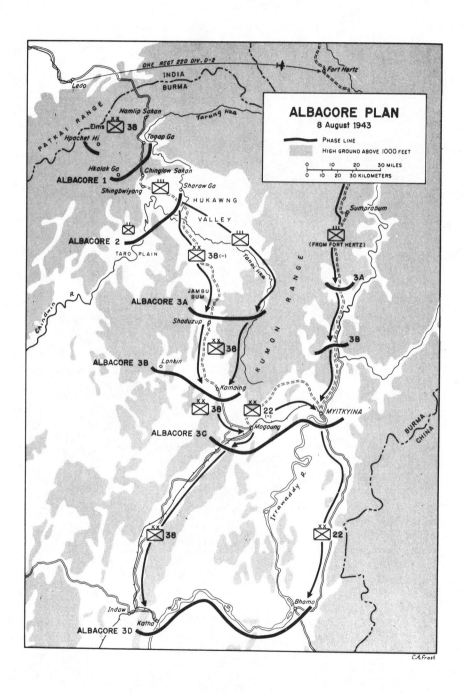

ALBACORE PLAN
8 August 1943

PHASE LINE
HIGH GROUND ABOVE 1000 FEET

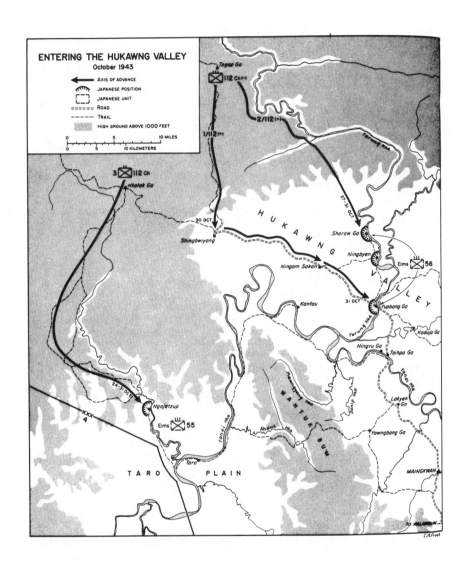

ENTERING THE HUKAWNG VALLEY
October 1943

AXIS OF ADVANCE
JAPANESE POSITION
JAPANESE UNIT
ROAD
TRAIL
HIGH GROUND ABOVE 1000 FEET

0   5   10 MILES
0   5   10 KILOMETERS

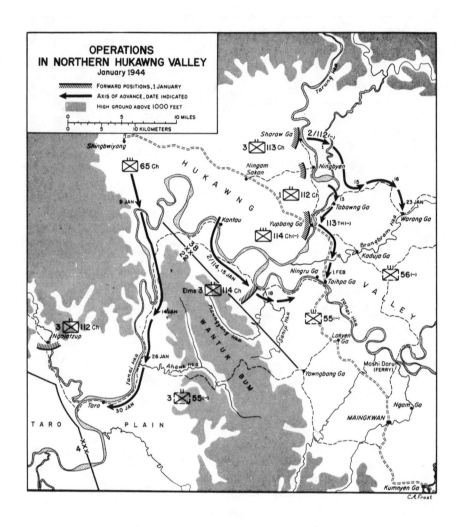

OPERATIONS
IN NORTHERN HUKAWNG VALLEY
January 1944

FORWARD POSITIONS, 1 JANUARY
AXIS OF ADVANCE, DATE INDICATED
HIGH GROUND ABOVE 1000 FEET

0   5   10 MILES
0   5   10 KILOMETERS

C.A. Frost

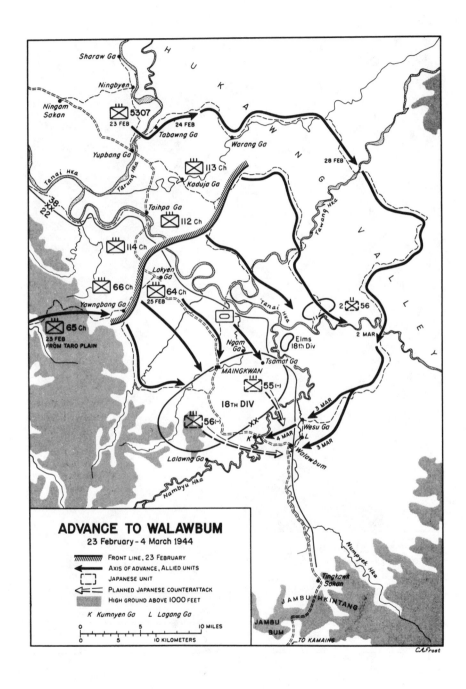

ADVANCE TO WALAWBUM
23 February – 4 March 1944

/////////	FRONT LINE, 23 FEBRUARY
⬛➡	AXIS OF ADVANCE, ALLIED UNITS
⬜	JAPANESE UNIT
⬅	PLANNED JAPANESE COUNTERATTACK
▨	HIGH GROUND ABOVE 1000 FEET

K Kumnyen Ga   L Lagang Ga

0 ———— 5 ———— 10 MILES
0 ———— 5 ———— 10 KILOMETERS

C.A.Frost

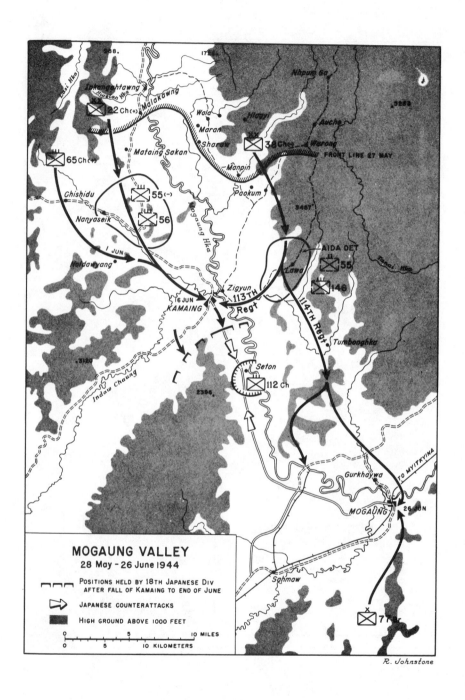

988.

1738.

Tani Hka

Ipkangahtawng

Nhpum Ga

Hwelon Hka

Malakawng

5883.

22 Ch(+)

Wala

Hkagyi

Auche

111

Maran

Sharaw

WARONG

65 Ch(+)

Mataing Sakan

Manpin

FRONT LINE 27 MAY

38 Cheg

Chishidu

55 (-)

Paokum

3487

Nanyaseik

56

AIDA DET

Lawa

55

Naldawyang

I JUN

148

Zigyun

6 JUN

113 TH

KAMAING

Regt

114TH Regt

Tumbonghka

3120

Seton

Indaw Chaung

2396.

112 Ch

Gurkhaywa

TO MYITKYINA

MOGAUNG

26 JUN

Sahmaw

MOGAUNG VALLEY
28 May – 26 June 1944

POSITIONS HELD BY 18TH JAPANESE DIV
AFTER FALL OF KAMAING TO END OF JUNE

JAPANESE COUNTERATTACKS

HIGH GROUND ABOVE 1000 FEET

77 Br

0   5   10 MILES

0   5   10 KILOMETERS

R. Johnstone

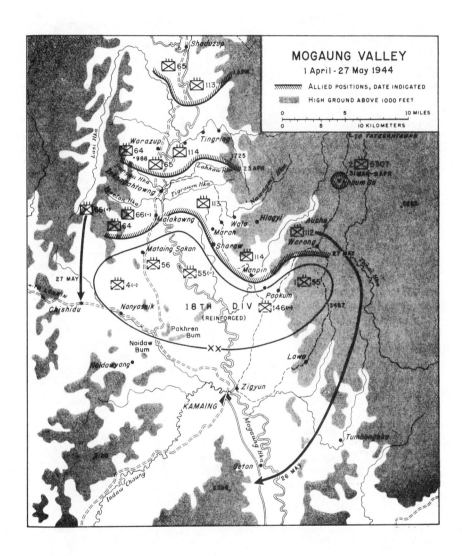

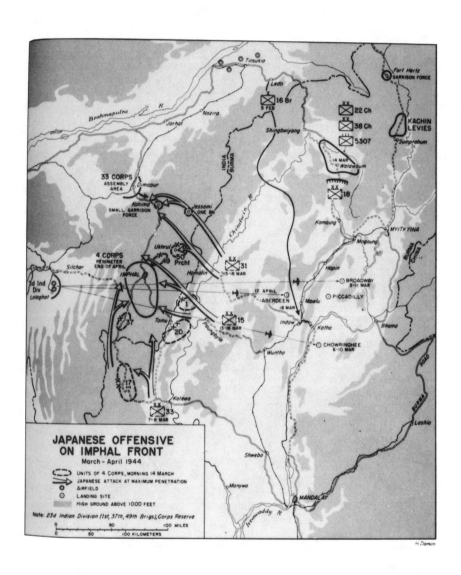

**JAPANESE OFFENSIVE
ON IMPHAL FRONT**
March – April 1944

UNITS OF 4 CORPS, MORNING 14 MARCH
JAPANESE ATTACK AT MAXIMUM PENETRATION
AIRFIELD
LANDING SITE
HIGH GROUND ABOVE 1000 FEET

Note: 23d Indian Division (1st, 37th, 49th Brigs), Corps Reserve

0   50   100 MILES
0   50   100 KILOMETERS

H. Damon

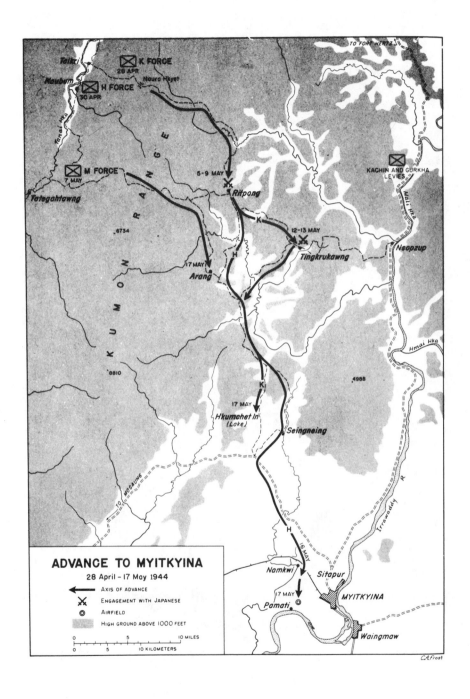

Taikri
Maubyin
K FORCE
28 APR
Nauro Hkyet
H FORCE
30 APR
Tanai Hka
Tanai Hka
M FORCE
7 MAY
Fatagahtawng
KUMON RANGE
.6734
5-9 MAY
Ritpong
K
12-13 MAY
Tingkrukawng
Nsopzup
H
17 MAY
Arang
.8810
TO FORT HERTZ
KACHIN AND GURKHA
LEVIES
Mali Hka
Hmai Hka
.4988
K
17 MAY
Hkumchet In
(Loke)
Seingneing
TO MOGAUNG
Irrawaddy R.
H
16 MAY
Namkwi
Sitapur
MYITKYINA
17 MAY
Pamati
Waingmaw

ADVANCE TO MYITKYINA

28 April – 17 May 1944

⟵ AXIS OF ADVANCE

✖ ENGAGEMENT WITH JAPANESE

◎ AIRFIELD

HIGH GROUND ABOVE 1000 FEET

| 0 | 5 | 10 MILES |
| 0 | 5 | 10 KILOMETERS |

C.A.Frost

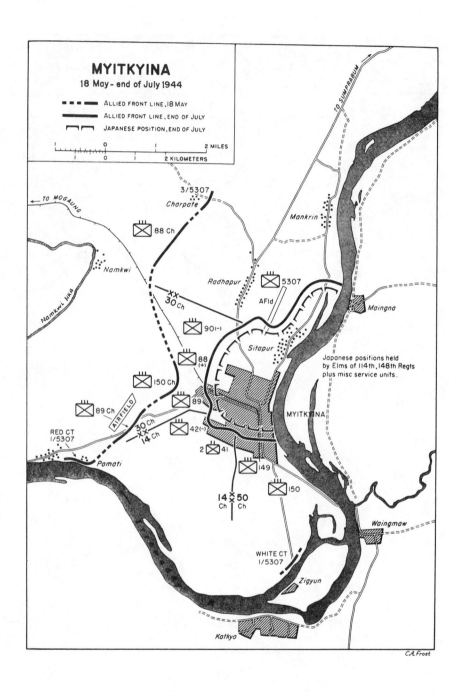

MYITKYINA
18 May - end of July 1944

ALLIED FRONT LINE, 18 MAY
ALLIED FRONT LINE, END OF JULY
JAPANESE POSITION, END OF JULY

0   2 MILES
0   1   2 KILOMETERS

TO MOGAUNG

TO SUMPRABUM

3/5307
Charpate
88 Ch
Namkwi
Namkwi Hka
Radhapur
5307
AFld
Mankrin
Maingna
XX
30 Ch
90 (-)
Sitapur
Japanese positions held
by Elms of 114th, 148th Regts
plus misc service units.
88 (+)
150 Ch
89 Ch
AIRFIELD
89
MYITKYINA
RED CT
1/5307
30 Ch
XX
14 Ch
42 (-)
Pamati
2   41
149
14 X 50
Ch Ch
150
Waingmaw
WHITE CT
1/5307
Zigyun
Katkya

C.A. Frost

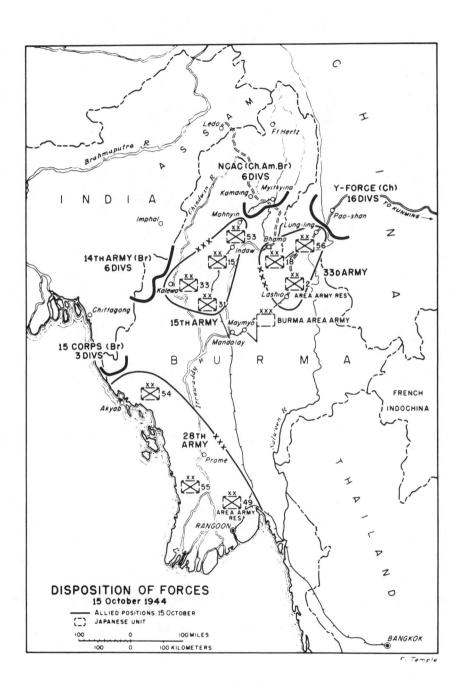

C

H

I

N

A

ASSAM

INDIA

BURMA

THAILAND

FRENCH
INDOCHINA

Brahmaputra R.

Ledo

Ft Hertz

NCAC(Ch,Am,Br)
6 DIVS

Chindwin R.

Kamaing

Myitkyina

Y-FORCE (Ch)
16 DIVS

TO KUNMING

Imphal

Mohnyin

Pao-shan

Lung-ling

XXX 53

Bhama

XX 56

14TH ARMY (Br)
6 DIVS

Indaw

XX 15

XX 18

XXXX

33D ARMY

XX 33

Kalewa

Lashio

XX 2

AREA ARMY RES

XX 31

15TH ARMY

Maymyo

XXX

BURMA AREA ARMY

15 CORPS (Br)
3 DIVS

Mandalay

Chittagong

Irrawaddy R.

Salween R.

XX 54

Akyab

28TH
ARMY

XXX

Prome

XX 55

XX 49

AREA ARMY
RES

RANGOON

BANGKOK

DISPOSITION OF FORCES
15 October 1944

——— ALLIED POSITIONS,15 OCTOBER
[‾‾] JAPANESE UNIT

100   0   100 MILES

100   0   100 KILOMETERS

F. Temple

Index